Ranger Rick's NatureScope

DIVING INTO OCEANS

National Wildlife Federation

LEARNING
TRIANGLE
PRESS

*Connecting
kids, parents, and teachers
through learning*

An imprint of McGraw-Hill
New York San Francisco Washington, D.C. Auckland Bogotá Caracas
Lisbon London Madrid Mexico City Milan Montreal New Delhi
San Juan Singapore Sydney Tokyo Toronto

Library of Congress Cataloging-in-Publication Data

Diving into oceans / National Wildlife Federation
      p.   cm. — (Ranger Rick's naturescope)
    Includes bibliographical references (p. 92).
    ISBN 0-07-047097-9 (pbk.)
    1. Oceanography I. National Wildlife Federation. II. Series.
  GC21.D49   1997
  551.46—dc21   97-35983
                                        CIP

McGraw-Hill

*A Division of The **McGraw·Hill** Companies*

NATIONAL WILDLIFE FEDERATION®

NatureScope® is published by Learning Triangle Press, an imprint of McGraw-Hill. Copyright 1998, 1989 by the National Wildlife Federation. All rights reserved. Permission is granted, without written request, to copy pages specified as "Copycat Pages," as well as those sections of the text specifically designated for student use. The reproduction of any other parts of this book is strictly prohibited without written permission from the publisher, McGraw-Hill. The publisher takes no responsibility for the use of any materials or methods described in this book, nor for the products thereof.

1 2 3 4 5 6 7 8 9 JDL/JDL 9 0 2 1 0 9 8 7

ISBN 0-07-047097-9

NatureScope® was originally conceived by National Wildlife Federation's School Programs Editorial Staff, under the direction of Judy Braus, Editor. Special thanks to all of the Editorial Staff, Scientific, Educational Consultants and Contributors who brought this series of eighteen publications to life.

NATIONAL WILDLIFE FEDERATION EDITORIAL STAFF
Creative Services Manager: Sharon Schiliro
Editor, Ranger Rick® magazine: Gerry Bishop
Director, Classroom-related Programs: Margaret Tunstall
Contributors: Salt Marsh Secrets by Mary E. Young;
Marine Pollution: A Critical Coastal Issue by John A. Tiedemann;
Creatures of the Sea, and Currents by Hamline University

McGRAW-HILL EDP STAFF
Acquisitions Editor: Judith Terrill-Breuer
Editorial Supervisor: Patricia V. Amoroso
Production Supervisor: Claire Stanley
Designer: York Production Services
Cover Design: David Saylor

McGraw-Hill books are available at special quantity discounts to use as premiums and sales promotions, or for use in corporate training programs. For more information, please write to the Director of Special Sales, McGraw-Hill, 11 West 19th Street, New York, NY 10011. Or contact your local bookstore.

Printed and bound by the John D. Lucas Printing Company.
This book is printed on recycled and acid-free paper.

TM and ® designate trademarks of National Wildlife Federation and are used, under license, by The McGraw-Hill Companies, Inc.

RRNS

OTHER TITLES IN *RANGER RICK'S NATURESCOPE*

AMAZING MAMMALS, PART I
AMAZING MAMMALS, PART II
ASTRONOMY ADVENTURES
BIRDS, BIRDS, BIRDS
DIGGING INTO DINOSAURS
DISCOVERING DESERTS
ENDANGERED SPECIES: WILD & RARE
GEOLOGY: THE ACTIVE EARTH

INCREDIBLE INSECTS
LET'S HEAR IT FOR HERPS
POLLUTION: PROBLEMS & SOLUTIONS
RAIN FORESTS: TROPICAL TREASURES
TREES ARE TERRIFIC!
WADING INTO WETLANDS
WILD ABOUT WEATHER
WILD & CRAFTY

GOAL

Ranger Rick's NatureScope is a creative education series dedicated to inspiring in children an understanding and appreciation of the natural world while developing the skills they will need to make responsible decisions about the environment.

TABLE OF CONTENTS

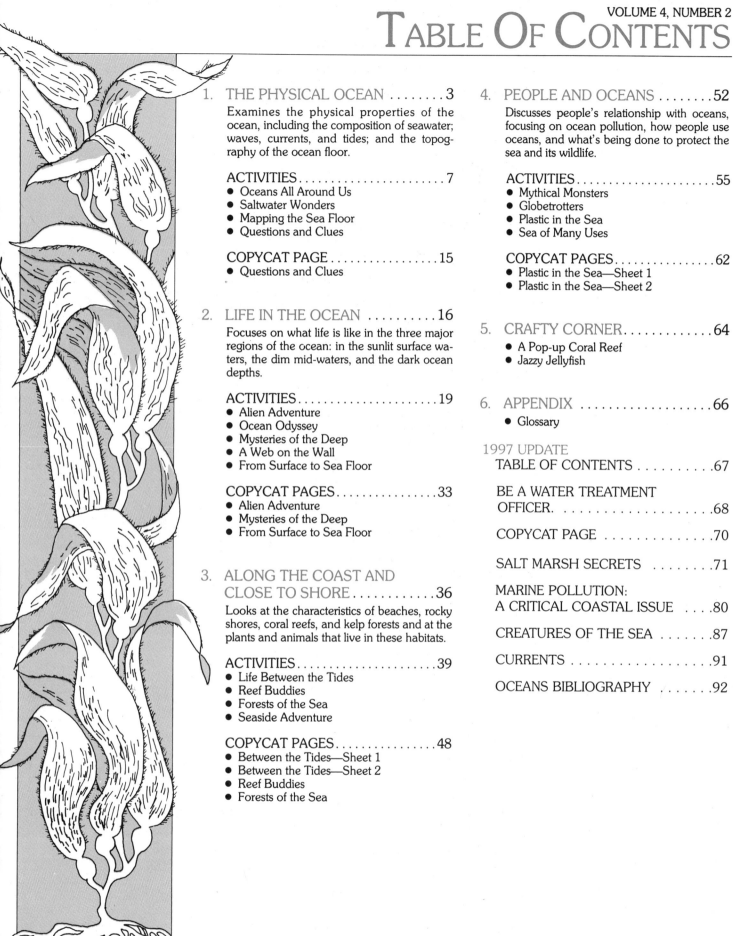

1. THE PHYSICAL OCEAN 3
Examines the physical properties of the ocean, including the composition of seawater; waves, currents, and tides; and the topography of the ocean floor.

ACTIVITIES 7
• Oceans All Around Us
• Saltwater Wonders
• Mapping the Sea Floor
• Questions and Clues

COPYCAT PAGE 15
• Questions and Clues

2. LIFE IN THE OCEAN 16
Focuses on what life is like in the three major regions of the ocean: in the sunlit surface waters, the dim mid-waters, and the dark ocean depths.

ACTIVITIES 19
• Alien Adventure
• Ocean Odyssey
• Mysteries of the Deep
• A Web on the Wall
• From Surface to Sea Floor

COPYCAT PAGES 33
• Alien Adventure
• Mysteries of the Deep
• From Surface to Sea Floor

3. ALONG THE COAST AND
CLOSE TO SHORE 36
Looks at the characteristics of beaches, rocky shores, coral reefs, and kelp forests and at the plants and animals that live in these habitats.

ACTIVITIES 39
• Life Between the Tides
• Reef Buddies
• Forests of the Sea
• Seaside Adventure

COPYCAT PAGES 48
• Between the Tides—Sheet 1
• Between the Tides—Sheet 2
• Reef Buddies
• Forests of the Sea

4. PEOPLE AND OCEANS 52
Discusses people's relationship with oceans, focusing on ocean pollution, how people use oceans, and what's being done to protect the sea and its wildlife.

ACTIVITIES 55
• Mythical Monsters
• Globetrotters
• Plastic in the Sea
• Sea of Many Uses

COPYCAT PAGES 62
• Plastic in the Sea—Sheet 1
• Plastic in the Sea—Sheet 2

5. CRAFTY CORNER 64
• A Pop-up Coral Reef
• Jazzy Jellyfish

6. APPENDIX 66
• Glossary

1997 UPDATE
TABLE OF CONTENTS 67

BE A WATER TREATMENT
OFFICER. .68

COPYCAT PAGE 70

SALT MARSH SECRETS 71

MARINE POLLUTION:
A CRITICAL COASTAL ISSUE 80

CREATURES OF THE SEA 87

CURRENTS 91

OCEANS BIBLIOGRAPHY 92

A CLOSE-UP LOOK AT DIVING INTO OCEANS

Looking at the Table of Contents, you can see we've divided *Diving into Oceans* into four chapters (each of which deals with a broad ocean theme), a craft section, and an appendix. The four chapters include *background information* that explains concepts and vocabulary, *activities* that relate to each chapter theme, and *Copycat Pages* that reinforce many of the concepts introduced in the activities.

You can choose single activity ideas or teach each chapter as a unit. Either way, each activity stands by itself and includes teaching objectives, a list of materials needed, suggested age groups, subjects covered, and a step-by-step explanation of how to do the activity. (The objectives, materials, age groups, and subjects are highlighted in the left-hand margin for easy reference.)

AGE GROUPS

The suggested age groups are:
- Primary (grades K–2)
- Intermediate (grades 3–5)
- Advanced (grades 6–8)

Each chapter begins with primary activities and ends with intermediate and advanced activities. But don't feel bound by the grade levels we suggest. You'll be able to adapt many of the activities to fit your particular age group and needs.

OUTDOOR ACTIVITIES

We've included several outdoor activities in this issue. These are coded in the chapters in which they appear with this symbol:

COPYCAT PAGES

The *Copycat Pages* supplement the activities and include ready-to-copy games, puzzles, coloring pages, and/or worksheets. Look at the bottom of each Copycat Page for the name and page number of the activity that it goes with. *Answers to all Copycat Pages are in the texts of the activities.*

WHAT'S AT THE END

The fifth section, *Crafty Corner,* will give you some art and craft ideas that complement many of the activities in the first four chapters. And the last section, the *Appendix,* is loaded with reference suggestions that include books, films, and posters. The *Appendix* also has a glossary and suggestions for where to get more ocean information.

THE PHYSICAL OCEAN

When the Earth first formed from a swirling, thick cloud of gas and dust more than four billion years ago, there wasn't an ocean on the planet. Instead, the Earth's surface was a rocky war zone. Violent volcanic eruptions showered the atmosphere and landscape with molten rock and with steam and other hot gases.

So when and how did our oceans form? That's a question that still puzzles scientists. One of the most widely believed theories claims that the steam and other gases released from these early volcanic eruptions formed a thick layer of clouds around the Earth, eventually causing torrents of rain to fall for hundreds of millions of years. According to this theory, the super rainstorm filled the ocean basins by about 3.5 billion years ago.

However, a recent theory states the oceans might *not* have formed billions of years ago. Louis Frank, a respected space scientist, thinks the oceans have been filling gradually—the result of a four-billion-year-long bombardment of 100-ton icy comets. This bombardment, he says, is still occurring today. As these comets crash into the atmosphere, they instantly vaporize, adding moisture to the air that eventually falls as rain or snow. Frank says the amount of moisture—about one ten-thousandth of an inch of water each year—is "indistinguishable from the annual rainfall." But if this rate has been constant for the past four billion years or so, it would have produced enough water to have filled up the oceans.

Controversy about the ocean is nothing new. For thousands of years people have debated everything from why the ocean is salty to what causes tides. And although there are still dozens of marine mysteries waiting to be solved, scientists have come a long way in understanding what really makes the ocean "tick."

ALL ABOUT SEAWATER

If you look at a globe, you'll see that there are four major oceans in the world, together covering about 71 percent of the Earth's surface. From largest to smallest, there's the Pacific, the Atlantic, the Indian, and the Arctic. But if you take a closer look, you'll see that all of these oceans are connected, forming one giant world ocean. Although there are some physical differences among ocean areas, the ocean waters of the world mix to form one amazingly uniform pot of salty soup.

Salt in the Sea: If you let a sample of ocean water evaporate, you'll see a residue of salt left behind. Most of this residue would be sodium chloride—the same kind of salt that we use on our food. But many other salts, including those of magnesium, calcium, and potassium, are also in seawater.

How do these salts get into the ocean? As water flows across the land, it picks up and dissolves salts from soil and rock and eventually deposits them into the ocean. (Many scientists think most of the Earth's original salts formed as a result of chemical reactions that occurred during volcanic activity billions of years ago.)

But the salt cycle is not a one-way path. If it were, the ocean would continue to get saltier every day, which it doesn't. Instead, salts are constantly "leaving" ocean waters: becoming part of the ocean floor, getting carried into the atmosphere on evaporating water droplets, and being absorbed by sea organisms. All salts, even those that leave, eventually get recycled back into the ocean—sometimes millions of years later—through geological, biological, and chemical processes.

(continued next page)

Gold and Gas: Although salts are the major dissolved solids in ocean water, they aren't the only ones. Seawater also contains traces of gold, silver, and all the chemical elements that make up the Earth's crust. When scientists refer to the *salinity* of the ocean, they are talking about the amount of all dissolved solids in ocean water, including the trace elements and minerals that are not salts.

Gases, such as oxygen and carbon dioxide, are also dissolved in the ocean and can move back and forth between the sea and the air. For example, some oxygen from the air diffuses into surface waters.

Cold, Cold Water: If you live on the Gulf Coast, you might not think of ocean water as being frigid. But most ocean water *is* cold. Only eight percent of all the ocean water in the world is warmer than 50° F. And more than half is colder than 36° F.

The warmest ocean waters are surface waters. That's because most of the energy from the sun that hits the ocean is absorbed in the top few inches. Below the surface, ocean temperatures can vary greatly. As a general rule, the lower you go, the colder it gets. And in the deepest parts, the water is near or below 32° F.

The Colder the Denser: Water behaves in certain ways depending on its temperature and salinity. Cold water is denser than warm water because the molecules are packed more closely together in a given volume. Salinity also increases density. So water that is cold and salty tends to sink under warmer, less salty water. And this "sinking" is a major triggering force of ocean currents. (See "Hot and Cold Currents" below.)

Pounds of Pressure: Water is heavy, and the deeper you dive into ocean waters, the more pressure you'll feel. Animals and plants that live deep in the ocean are adapted to this pressure, but people aren't. And that's why they need special pressurized diving suits and capsules to explore ocean depths.

THE MOTION OF THE OCEAN

Ocean water is always on the move—from the constant tumble of waves along the shore to the quiet ebb of the tide. Here's a closer look at ocean motions:

RIVERS IN THE SEA

The Gulf Stream, Kuroshio, North Atlantic Drift, Labrador Current, and Alaska Drift are all examples of *currents*, or "rivers of water," that flow through the ocean in certain directions. Ocean currents can be caused by two things: steady winds blowing across the ocean's surface and differences in temperature and salinity of ocean waters.

Steady Winds: Most of the world's wind-generated currents are caused by the *prevailing winds*—winds that blow continuously in the same general direction. The two most predictable prevailing winds are the trade winds, which generally blow from east to west toward the equator, and the westerlies, which usually blow from west to east in the middle latitudes. One of the strongest wind-generated currents is the West Wind Drift, which travels around the Antarctic continent. (The direction that prevailing winds blow, and thus currents flow, are influenced by the rotation of the Earth. For more about prevailing winds, see page 15 of *NatureScope—Wild About Weather* [Vol. 1, No. 3].)

Hot and Cold Currents: Temperature currents are caused by the differences in temperature between the cold waters of the poles and the warm waters near the equator. Cold-water currents occur as the cold water at the poles sinks and slowly moves toward the equator. Warm-water currents travel out from the equator along the surface, flowing toward the poles to replace the sinking cold water.

NWF file

Mixing and Warming: Currents—especially cold-water currents—circulate ocean water around the world and help mix it vertically, replenishing oxygen supplies in the lower depths and bringing nutrients to the surface. Warm ocean currents bring moderate temperatures to areas that would normally be much colder. For example, the Gulf Stream flows from the Gulf of Mexico, past the East Coast of the United States, to northern Europe. Without the Gulf Stream, England and the other European countries would be as cold as Canada.

WAVE ACTION

It's usually impossible to see a current from the ocean's surface. But that's not the case with waves. Waves constantly cause ocean waters to rise and fall as they transfer energy from one part of the ocean to another.

What's a Wave?: It's easy to get confused when talking about waves because the word *wave* is used to describe an actual swell of water, as well as energy that moves through water. Waves can be caused by wind, volcanic activity, or earthquakes, but wind-generated waves are the most common. (For more about waves generated by volcanic activity or earthquakes, see "Tsunamis" on page 8 of *NatureScope—Geology: The Active Earth* [Vol. 3, No. 2].)

Waves differ from currents in that they usually do not move ocean water forward. Instead, they transfer energy from one part of the ocean to another, and as they do this the ocean water moves up and down. A gull sitting on the surface of the water will bob up and down as a wave passes through the water, but it won't move forward.

Breakers on the Beach: Ocean waves *do* move water forward when they hit the shore. That's because when a wave reaches land, it starts to drag on the bottom. You can tell when this is happening just by watching an approaching wave. As the bottom of the wave begins to drag on the ocean bottom, the lower part of the wave slows down. But the top keeps going until it topples over, causing the wave to "break" on the beach. These breakers pitch water, as well as sand and other types of sediment stirred up from the bottom, onto the beach.

TIDE TALK

Although the wind plays a big part in most ocean motion, it does not cause *tides*—the slow, periodic rise and fall of ocean waters. Tides are mainly caused by the gravitational attraction of the moon and sun on the Earth.

Moon Muscle: The gravitational forces of the moon and sun are constantly pulling at the water, air, and land on Earth. And because the moon is so much closer to the Earth than the sun is, it exerts a much stronger gravitational pull on the Earth than the sun does. In fact, it pulls more than two times as hard on the Earth than the sun does.

This "moon muscle" is the main reason we experience tides. But the rotation of the Earth and moon also have an affect on them, as does the size, shape, and depth of ocean basins. For example, along the Atlantic Ocean, there are usually two high and two low tides a day. But the Mediterranean Sea doesn't have much tide action at all. And some places along the coast of Alaska and the Gulf of Mexico only experience one high tide and one low tide each day.

Highs and Lows: Every other week, tides are much higher or much lower than at other times. This is due to the relative positions of the sun, moon, and Earth. For example, when the sun, moon, and Earth are aligned, the highest high tides, called *spring tides*, occur. That's because both the sun and moon are pulling ocean water in the same direction. But when the moon and sun are at right angles to each other, their gravitational pulls partially cancel each other, and the lowest high tides, called *neap tides*, occur.

(continued next page)

VOYAGE TO THE BOTTOM OF THE SEA

About 71 percent of the Earth's surface is under the oceans. What does this surface look like? Until recently, no one really knew for sure. But in the last century, scientists have mapped the land under the sea and have discovered that, contrary to what people once thought, ocean landscapes are anything but dull.

A Shelf Offshore: From the edge of most continents, the land forms a gently sloping ledge, called the *continental shelf.* The width of the shelf and the depth of the water above it vary throughout the world. Off some continents, the surface of the shelf is covered with hills, valleys, and troughs. But in other areas it's level.

The continental shelf is covered with a rich deposit of sediment, which includes the remains of dead plants and animals as well as river-dumped sediment made up of tiny bits of clay, sand, shells, minerals, and other particles.

Down the Slope: At the edge of a continental shelf, the land takes a plunge, dropping steeply toward the deep-ocean bottom. This *continental slope* is much steeper than the shelf and, in many areas, is cut by deep canyons and twisted gorges—some of which rival the Grand Canyon in steepness and depth. Some scientists think that the canyons form as sediments from the continental shelf mix with ocean water and grind their way down the continental slope. At the bottom of the slope, these sediments spread out to form the *continental rise*—an apron of sediment that extends to the deep-ocean bottom.

The Deep, Dark Depths: Beyond the shelf, slope, and rise—at depths of more than 13,000 feet—are wide, slightly rolling plains. These *abyssal plains* cover more than 60 percent of the sea floor, which is about half of the Earth's surface, and they are covered with a thick layer of deep-ocean sediment. Much of this sediment is made up of microscopic shells and other organic materials from plants and animals that have died and slowly settled to the bottom. But some of the sediment is made up of dust from outer space and from continental runoff that is carried from the shelf and slope by currents.

Peaks and Valleys: Rising from the abyssal plains are volcanic hills, valleys, peaks, and mountain ranges. Many of these landforms are striking. For example, Mauna Kea in Hawaii is an inactive volcano that rises more than 33,000 feet straight up from the sea floor, making it taller than Mt. Everest. And the Mid-Atlantic Ridge, a deep-sea mountain range, runs from Iceland to Antarctica—a distance of more than 10,000 miles.

Deep-sea trenches are also a common ocean-floor feature in some ocean areas—especially in the Pacific. These deep valleys separate the continental slope from the deep-ocean basins, and are the deepest spots on Earth.

By studying deep-sea landforms, scientists have discovered more about earthquakes, volcanoes, and plate tectonics. (For information about the origin of these landforms and the theory of plate tectonics, see pages 3–5 of *NatureScope—Geology: The Active Earth* [Vol. 3, No. 2].)

* *Note:* Because the horizontal and vertical axes don't have the same interval scales, the steepness of the slopes on the diagram has been exaggerated.

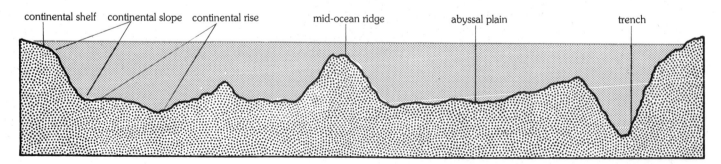

continental shelf   continental slope   continental rise   mid-ocean ridge   abyssal plain   trench

Oceans All Around Us

Discuss oceans, try some demonstrations, and sing a song.

Objectives:
Explain that most ocean water is very cold, that oceans cover most of the Earth, and that all the oceans are connected. Name the oceans.

Ages:
Primary

Materials:
- *construction paper*
- *toothpicks*
- *glue*
- *scissors*
- *chalkboard or easel paper*
- *globe*
- *modeling clay*
- *tape*
- *water*
- *three bowls*
- *ice cubes*
- *thermometer*

Subject:
Science

W hich covers more of the Earth's surface—land or ocean? In this activity the kids in your group will find out while learning more about the ocean in general.

Before you get started, make four small flags by gluing small triangular or rectangular pieces of construction paper to four different toothpicks. Number the flags from one to four. Also make an equal number of one-inch brown "land" and blue "ocean" squares by cutting apart different-colored sheets of construction paper. (For a globe that's twelve inches in diameter, you should make one hundred of each color.) Then make some smaller "land" and "ocean" pieces by cutting a few of the squares in half. The kids will be covering a globe with these squares and half-squares later.

Now begin by asking the kids what they know about the ocean and listing their ideas on a chalkboard or sheet of easel paper. Then discuss oceans in greater detail by doing each of the demonstrations below. (You may want to spread the demonstrations out over a few days.)

Afterward review what the kids have learned by singing the song on page 8. Then ask them if there's anything they'd like to change or add to the list they made earlier. (For more about life in the sea, see chapters two and three.)

DO SOME DEMONSTRATIONS

ONE WORLD OCEAN

Begin by showing the kids a globe and pointing out your location on it. Then point out and name each of the four major oceans. (Pacific, Arctic, Atlantic, and Indian) As you name each ocean, put a small lump of clay somewhere on it. Then stick one of the numbered flags you made earlier into the clay. You should number the oceans in such a way that the kids can travel from 1 to 4 without passing through the same ocean twice. One way to do this is to number the oceans as follows: 1—Pacific, 2—Arctic, 3—Atlantic, 4—Indian.

Now ask the kids if they think it's possible to travel completely around the world without touching land. Then challenge one or two kids to trace a path from ocean to ocean by going in order from flags 1 to 4 and then from flag 4 directly to flag 1. (Make sure they travel only across water.)

Afterward point out that even though different areas of the ocean have different names, they're all connected into one giant ocean.

THE WATER PLANET

Have the kids look at the globe for a few minutes and decide if they think the Earth is covered mostly by ocean or land. Then tell them that they're going to compare the amount of land with the amount of ocean.

First divide the group into two teams—the "Landlubbers" and the "Sea Dogs." Give each child on each team some of the colored squares you made earlier and give one child on each team all of the half-squares. Give all the Landlubbers land squares and all the Sea Dogs ocean squares. Be sure to pass out *all* of the squares. Explain to the kids that you've passed out an equal number of squares to both teams.

Now have the Landlubbers work in pairs to tape their squares in rows over all

the land on the globe. (Tell them to cover lakes and rivers too.) Have the person with half-squares go last to fill in any gaps. Then let the Sea Dogs cover as much of the ocean as they can with their squares, again having the person with half-squares go last. (*Note:* Explain to the kids that their squares should touch sides but not overlap. It's OK if there are small gaps between the squares on the globe. And it's OK if their squares are partly on land and partly on ocean as long as each Landlubber square is mostly on land and each Sea Dog square is mostly on ocean. For example, the Landlubbers shouldn't cover small islands in the ocean—they should leave them to the Sea Dogs.)

When all of the kids have finished taping their squares to the globe, have them take another look at it. Ask them how much land they can see and how much ocean. (Almost all of the land should be covered but most of the ocean should be showing.) Then ask them again if the Earth's surface is covered mostly by ocean or land. (ocean) Is there just a little more ocean than land or a lot more? (a lot more)

"The Water Planet" was adapted with permission from *Holt Science,* published by Holt, Rinehart and Winston, 1986.

COLD, COLDER, COLDEST

Place two bowls in the middle of a small table and label one A and the other B. Fill bowl A with water that's between 65° and 75° F. Fill bowl B with water that's below 36° F. Place bowl B inside a second, larger bowl that's filled with ice cubes.

Now have the kids gather around the table. Tell them that the two water samples represent water taken from different parts of the ocean. Have them take turns feeling the temperature of each sample by putting their fingers into each of the bowls. Which sample do the kids think is most like temperatures way down deep in the ocean? (sample B) Which do they think is most like temperatures in most of the ocean? (sample B)

Afterward point out that shallow, coastal waters that people go swimming in are warmer than most ocean waters and can be as warm or even warmer than the water in bowl A was. So can surface waters in the open ocean. But most of the water in the ocean is very cold—as cold as or colder than sample B was.

Luise Woelflein

SING A SEA SONG

(Sing to the tune of "My Bonnie Lies over the Ocean.")

The Earth is all covered with ocean.
The Earth is all covered with sea.
The Earth is all covered with ocean.
More water than land, don't you see?

Chorus:
Water, water, there's water all over the world, the world.
Water, water, there's water all over the world.

So salty and cold is the ocean.
So salty and cold is the sea.
So salty and cold is the ocean.
Too cold and too salty for me.

Repeat chorus

Atlantic, Pacific, the Arctic,
And then there's the Indian too.
These oceans all cover our planet.
I named all of them, now can you?

Repeat chorus

Saltwater Wonders

Conduct some saltwater experiments.

Objective:
Describe several physical characteristics of the ocean.

Ages:
Intermediate and Advanced

Materials:
- *copies of pages 10 and 11*
- *scissors*
- *glue*
- *index cards*
- *aquarium, kosher, or canning salt*
- *airtight containers*
- *water*
- *paper and pencils*
- *for other materials, see suggestions listed with each experiment*

Subject:
Science

ere's a hands-on way for the kids in your group to discover some of the characteristics of seawater and to think about how these properties might affect life in the ocean. Before you get started, make copies of the experiments on pages 10 and 11, cut them apart, and glue each one to an index card. Also make up several gallons of salt water by mixing two tablespoons of aquarium, kosher, or canning salt per quart of water. (Aquarium salt is available in aquarium stores and some pet stores.) The kids will be using this salt water in many of the experiments. (It's referred to in the experiments as "saltwater solution.") Store the salt water in airtight containers in a cool place until the kids need it.

Now begin by dividing the kids into groups of four. Explain that each group is going to complete five different experiments. Tell them that before they do an experiment, they should read through the directions carefully. Then, using the questions under "Make a Prediction," they should write down on a sheet of paper what they think is going to happen. Next they should do the experiment and record their results. Afterward they should answer the questions listed under "Brain Busters."

Once everyone has had a chance to finish experiment #1, get all the kids back together and talk about the results and the questions. Use the information under "What Should Have Happened," below, to help with the discussion. Then let the kids start working on the next experiment. (*Note:* Depending on how much time you have, you might want to do these experiments as demonstrations and then discuss them with the kids.)

Several of these demonstrations were adapted with permission from *Living in Water,* an aquatic science curriculum published by the National Aquarium in Baltimore and supported by National Science Foundation Grant no. MDR 8470190.

(continued next page)

WHAT SHOULD HAVE HAPPENED

1. **Under Pressure:** The middle jet of water should have traveled farther than the top jet, and the bottom jet of water should have traveled farthest of all. Explain that water near the bottom of the milk carton is under more pressure than the water at the top because it has the weight of all the water on top of it. In the ocean, water pressure also increases with depth and in the deep ocean the pressure can be tremendous. At 30,000 feet the water pressure can be as great as having the weight of an elephant pushing against every square inch of your body! Life in the deep ocean is adapted to these conditions. (For more about life in the deep sea, see chapter two.)

2. **Hot and Cold:** The warm, colored salt water (solution 1) should have floated on top of the cold salt water (solution A). Almost all of the colored, cold salt water (solution 2) should have sunk to the bottom of the warm salt water (solution B). Explain that warm water is less dense than cold water and so it floats on top. Because cold water is denser than warm water, it sinks to the bottom. In the ocean, the warmest water is found at the surface and the water at the bottom of the ocean is very cold.

3. **The Salty Sea:** The colored, extra-salty water (solution 1) should have sunk to the bottom of the uncolored salt water (solution B). The colored, less salty water (solution 2) should have floated on top of the uncolored, extra-salty water (solution A). Explain that the saltier water is, the denser it is. And denser water sinks through less dense water. For example, extra-salty water in the ocean tends to sink. And as fresh river water flows into the sea, it tends to stay near the surface—flowing over the saltier, denser water in the sea.

4. **The Current Connection:** Colored water from the ice cubes should have sunk straight to the bottom of the pan and then moved along the bottom toward the far end. Explain that the melting water sank because it was colder and saltier and therefore denser.

As the ice cubes melted, the continuous stream of cold, salty water took the path of least resistance—it flowed along the bottom, underneath the less dense tap water. As ocean water is chilled at the polar regions, it sinks and flows toward the equator. These deep, cold-water currents are important in ocean circulation.

5. **Changing Temperatures:** The temperature of the air inside the first jar should have changed more rapidly than the temperature of the water inside the second jar. Explain that air changes temperature much more rapidly than water, so the temperature of the atmosphere changes more rapidly than that of the ocean. And air that blows across the sea tends to get warmed up or cooled down, depending on the temperature of the ocean. Therefore, coastal areas tend to have cooler temperatures in the summer and warmer temperatures in the winter than areas farther inland.

#1—Under Pressure

What You Need: empty 1-quart milk carton; 3 identical nails; ruler; empty margarine or small cottage cheese tub; cup or other container; 9 × 13″ baking pan; water

What To Do:

1. Open the entire top of the milk carton. Then push each of the 3 nails through the cardboard on one side of the carton so they are in a column (see diagram). Make sure that the bottom nail is at least 3 inches above the bottom and all the nails are at least 1 inch apart.
2. Lay the ruler down the middle of the pan so that the 12-inch end of the ruler is touching one end of the pan.
3. Place the empty margarine tub upside down in the baking pan at the 1-inch end of the ruler. (The margarine tub should be on top of the ruler.) Then set the milk carton on top of the tub so that the nails point toward the 12-inch end of the ruler (see diagram).

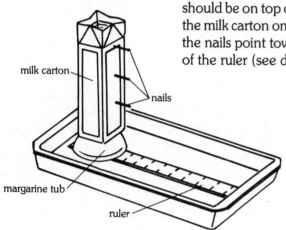

milk carton

nails

margarine tub

ruler

4. Fill the milk carton with water all the way to the top.
5. Pull all 3 nails out of the milk carton at the same time and then slowly pour water into the milk carton so that it's *always* filled.
6. As the water squirts out the nail holes, watch to see how far each jet goes.

Make a Prediction: Will the water coming from each hole travel the same distance or will some jets travel farther than others?

Brain Busters: What did you observe and why did it happen? What might this tell you about how pressure changes the deeper you go in the ocean?

#2—Hot and Cold

What You Need: 4 containers; clear plastic cup; measuring cup; measuring spoon; saltwater solution; aquarium, kosher, or canning salt; hot tap water; food coloring; medicine dropper; refrigerator

What To Do:

1. Pour 1 cup of saltwater solution into one of the containers and label it *solution A.* Then put it in a refrigerator for at least 2 hours.
2. Pour 1 cup of hot tap water into another container and add 1½ teaspoons of salt. Stir until all salt is dissolved. Label this container *solution B.*
3. Pour a small amount of *solution B* into a different container, add 4 or 5 drops of food coloring, and stir well. Label this container *solution 1.*
4. Fill the clear plastic cup with about 2 inches of *solution A.* Then drop about 20 drops of *solution 1* into the cup, using a medicine dropper. Watch to see what happens as the colored, warm salt water drips into the cold salt water. Then clean out the plastic cup.
5. Pour a small amount of *solution A* into a different container, add 4 or 5 drops of food coloring, and stir well. Label this container *solution 2.*
6. Fill the clear plastic cup with about 2 inches of *solution B.* Then drop about 20 drops of *solution 2* into the cup, using the dropper. Watch to see what happens as the colored, cold salt water drips into the warm salt water.

Make a Prediction: When you add warm salt water to chilled salt water, will it float at the surface, sink to the bottom, or mix right in? When you add chilled salt water to warm salt water, will it float, sink, or mix right in?

Brain Busters: What did you observe and why did it happen? Based on this experiment, where would you find the warmest water in the ocean—at the surface or close to the bottom?

#3—The Salty Sea

What You Need: 4 containers; clear plastic cup; measuring cup; saltwater solution; aquarium, kosher, or canning salt;

measuring spoon; food coloring; medicine dropper

What To Do:

1. Pour 1 cup of saltwater solution into each of 2 containers and label them *solution A* and *solution B.*
2. Make *solution A* extra salty by adding ¾ teaspoon of salt to it and stirring until the salt is dissolved.
3. Pour a small amount of *solution A* into another container, add 4 or 5 drops of food coloring, and stir well. Label this container *solution 1.*
4. Fill the clear plastic cup with about 2 inches of *solution B.* Then drop about 20 drops of *solution 1* into the container, using a medicine dropper. Watch to see what happens as the colored, extra-salty water drips into the less-salty water. Then clean out the plastic cup.
5. Pour a small amount of *solution B* into another container, add 4 or 5 drops of food coloring, and stir well. Label this container *solution 2.*
6. Fill the clear plastic cup with about 2 inches of *solution A.* Then drop about 20 drops of *solution 2* into the container, using a medicine dropper. Watch to see what happens as the colored salt water drips into the extra-salty water.

Make a Prediction: When you add extra-salty water to salty water will it float at the surface, sink to the bottom, or mix right in? When you add salty water to extra-salty water will it float at the surface, sink to the bottom, or mix right in?

Brain Busters: What did you observe and why did it happen? Based on this experiment, what do you think happens to river water, which is fresh water, as it flows into the sea? (Does it tend to float or does it sink to the bottom?)

#4—The Current Connection

What You Need: 9 × 13″ glass baking pan or other large, clear container; saltwater solution; container; plastic ice cube tray; food coloring; lukewarm tap water; freezer

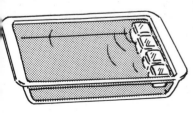

What To Do:

1. Add 4 or 5 drops of food coloring to a container of saltwater solution and stir well.
2. Fill 4 ice cube compartments in a plastic ice cube tray halfway with the colored salt water and freeze.
3. Fill a clear baking pan with lukewarm tap water. Then line up the 4 colored ice cubes along one end of the baking pan. (Use your finger to keep them from floating away.) Look into the pan from the side and watch what happens as the ice cubes melt.

Make a Prediction: As water from the ice cubes melts, will it sink straight to the bottom, float at the surface, or mix in?

Brain Busters: What did you observe and why did it happen? Based on this experiment, what do you think happens to ocean water as it's chilled at the polar regions?

#5—Changing Temperatures

What You Need: 2 large glass jars with lids; 2 thermometers that fit inside the jars; water; graph paper; refrigerator

What To Do:

1. Set a thermometer inside a glass jar and screw the lid on. A few minutes later, record the temperature on the thermometer. (This is the temperature of the air inside the jar.)
2. Fill the other glass jar with water that's the same temperature as the air inside the first jar. Put a thermometer in the jar and screw the lid on.
3. Put both jars in the refrigerator and record their temperatures every 3 minutes for 21 minutes. Graph the results.

Make a Prediction: After you set the jars in the refrigerator, will they change temperature at the same rate or will one change faster than the other?

Brain Busters: What did you observe and why did it happen? Based on this experiment, do you think the ocean changes temperature at the same rate as the air around it? How do you think temperatures along the coast might compare with an area 100 miles inland during the summer? During the winter?

Mapping the Sea Floor

Plot data for part of the floor of the Atlantic.

Objectives:
Explain how scientists measure ocean depths. Describe some features of the Atlantic Ocean's floor.

Ages:
Advanced

Materials:
- *chalkboard or easel paper*
- *copies of the data on page 13*
- *atlas*
- *graph paper*
- *tape*
- *pencils*
- *rulers*
- *markers*
- *physical globe or map of the world*

Subjects:
Science and Math

By plotting some ocean depth data, your group can "see" what the bottom of one section of the Atlantic Ocean is like. Before you get started, copy the diagram on the bottom of page 6 onto a chalkboard or sheet of easel paper and make copies of the "Ocean Depth Data" on page 13. Then begin by asking the kids what they think the bottom of the ocean is like. Is it flat or mountainous? Does it gradually become deeper and deeper or does it suddenly become very deep? Tell the kids that, by plotting some actual data scientists have collected, they'll find out what the bottom of one section of the Atlantic Ocean looks like.

Before you pass out the data, use the information under "Seeing the Sea Floor" on page 13 to discuss how people measure ocean depths. Then, to make sure the kids understand how echo sounding works, try some math problems with your group. Here's an example:

Approximately 1000 miles off the eastern coast of the United States, a sound impulse takes 6.92 seconds to travel from a boat to the sea floor and back. Given that the average speed of sound in seawater is approximately 5000 feet per second, about how deep is the ocean in this spot?
6.92 seconds ÷ 2 = 3.46 seconds one way
3.46 seconds × 5000 feet/second = 17,300 feet

Next pass out copies of the data on page 13 and tell the kids that it was collected along approximately 38°N latitude from the coast of the United States to the waters just offshore Europe. Have the kids look at an atlas and find where 38°N "hits" the United States and Europe. (Virginia and Portugal)

Depth of the Atlantic Ocean at 38°N

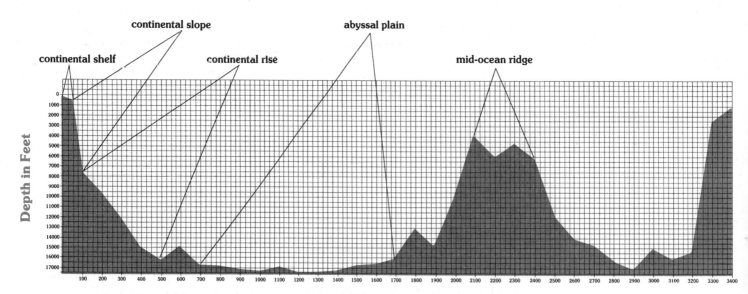

Distance from U.S. (nautical miles)	Depth (feet)
10	60
50	240
100	7500
200	9600
300	12000
400	14850
500	16278
600	14706
700	16650
800	16830
900	17160
1000	17298
1100	16830
1200	17460
1300	17310
1400	17298
1500	16698
1600	16500
1700	15978
1800	12978
1900	14790
2000	9840
2100	3798
2200	5952
2300	4620
2400	6150
2500	11940
2600	14070
2700	14658
2800	16398
2900	17172
3000	14880
3100	15858
3200	15240
3300	2430
3350	1770
3400	978

Data courtesy of the Defense Mapping Agency, Hydrographic/Topographic Center, Washington, DC.

Now pass out a pencil, ruler, and three sheets of graph paper to each child. Have the kids tape the three sheets of graph paper together lengthwise. Then have them label the vertical axis "Depth in Feet" and mark it in 1000-foot intervals from 0 to 17,500. Explain that the zero-depth mark (the surface of the water) should be at the top of their graphs (see diagram). Next have them label the horizontal axis "Distance from the U.S. in Nautical Miles" and mark it in 100-mile intervals from 0 (United States) to 3400 (Portugal). (A nautical mile is equal to approximately 1.15 statute miles—the miles we use on land.) Make sure they spread the miles out over the entire length of their three sheets of graph paper. And point out that the first two and last two points aren't at 100-mile intervals. Have the kids title their graphs "Depth of the Atlantic Ocean at 38° N." Then let the plotting begin!

As the kids plot each point, have them use a ruler to connect it to the last point they plotted. This will help them see what they're plotting as they go along. (To make it easier for the kids to plot, you might want to have them use their rulers as a guide between the vertical axis and the points they're plotting.)

When the kids have finished plotting and connecting all of the data, have them use markers to color in their graphs (see diagram). This will give them an idea of what the bottom of the Atlantic looks like along 38°N latitude. (*Note:* Because the horizontal and vertical axes don't have the same interval scales, the steepness of the slopes on the graph is exaggerated.)

Now tell the group that the picture they've drawn shows many of the same seafloor features that are found throughout the world's oceans. Show the kids the diagram you copied earlier and, using the information on page 6, go over the terms *continental shelf, continental slope, continental rise, abyssal plain,* and *mid-ocean ridge.* As you discuss each term have the kids find and label the corresponding section of their graphs (see diagram).

Afterward have the kids look at a physical globe or physical map of the world. (Physical globes and physical maps show relief.) Point out the mid-ocean ridge that runs down the middle of the Atlantic Ocean. Then have the kids look at the mountains in the other ocean basins. Also have them look for the continental shelves and other features of the ocean basins.

SEEING THE SEA FLOOR

Echoes from the Deep: For many years scientists have relied on a technique called *echo sounding* to determine ocean depths. Echo sounders are sonar devices that are attached to or built into ships' hulls. They send out regular and frequent pulses of sound that travel through the water and bounce off the ocean bottom. Underwater microphones pick up the returning echoes. And computers on board the ships can calculate how deep the water is in a certain area by measuring the time it takes the sound to return.

Ocean Floor "Photos": Recently scientists have begun using an additional kind of mapping system called *sidescan sonar.* Like echo sounding, sidescan sonar sends out sound signals that bounce off the ocean floor. But sidescan sonar can map much more of the sea floor at one time than any other kind of sonar. And instruments on board the ship primarily measure the character of the returning echoes, not the time it takes them to come back. By measuring the character of the echoes, graphic recorders on the ships can generate images of what the sea floor actually looks like in a particular area. Sand, mud, and rock, for example, all create different images. And by entering the data into computers, scientists can generate even clearer pictures of the sea floor. These pictures are similar to photographs.

Sidescan sonar is being used to map the coastal waters of the United States and has given scientists a more detailed "look" at the Mid-Atlantic Ridge, the East Pacific Rise, and other parts of the ocean bottom around the world. It was also used to find the *Titanic.*

Questions and Clues

Research some ocean topics and solve an ocean puzzle.

Objectives:
Define tides, currents, and waves. Discuss some ocean facts.

Ages:
Intermediate and Advanced

Materials:
- *copies of page 15*
- *chalkboard or easel paper*
- *reference books*
- *pencils*

Subject:
Science

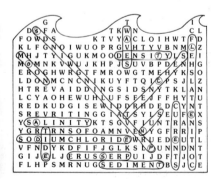

By using research to complete a word-find puzzle, the kids in your group will learn about waves, tides, currents, and more. Begin by dividing the group into four or five teams and explain that each team must research the following topics:

- tides, currents, and waves and what causes each phenomenon
- features of the ocean bottom
- salinity/composition of seawater

Tell the kids that the information they find about these topics will help them complete a puzzle.

Give the teams plenty of time to do their research, and encourage the kids in each team to split up the work. When all the teams are finished, pass out a copy of page 15 to each child. Explain that each person should use the information his or her team collected, along with the words at the bottom of the page, to complete each numbered clue on the page. Later they'll complete the word-find puzzle on the top half of the page. (Team members can work together to complete the clues. Point out that there are more words to choose from than blanks to fill in.)

When everyone has finished, go over the clues using the answers provided below. Also use the background information on pages 4–5 to talk about tides, waves, and currents with the kids. Then tell the kids that the word-find puzzle at the top of their Copycat Page contains all of the words and phrases that the kids used earlier to fill in the blanks in the clues. But each of these words and phrases is missing one or two letters. (For example, the word "currents" in the puzzle is written "curr○nts.") The kids should find each word, circle it, and write the missing letter

in the appropriate space. (For example, they would fill in "e" in the circled space in "currents.") Tell them not to look for the words they didn't use in the clues.

When the kids have found all the words and filled in their missing letters, tell them that the puzzle also contains three secret words. Then write the "Mystery Facts" listed below onto the chalkboard or a piece of easel paper and explain that each of the three secret words in the puzzle has something to do with one of the mystery facts.

To find the secret words, the kids should read all of the circled letters in order from left to right and top to bottom. They should be able to read the words "salt," "ocean," and "deepest." Then go over which secret word goes with which mystery fact. Explain that "salt" goes with 3½ percent, "ocean" goes with 71 percent, and "deepest" goes with Mariana Trench. Next tell the kids that, based on the research they did earlier, they should try to come up with a question that has something to do with each secret word. The answer to each question will be one of the mystery facts. For example, 3½ percent is the answer to the question, "By weight, what percentage of the ocean is made up of salt?" Seventy-one percent is the answer to the question, "What percentage of the Earth is covered with ocean?" And Mariana Trench is the answer to the question, "Where is the deepest place in the ocean?" (or "Where is the deepest spot on the surface of the Earth?")

MYSTERY FACTS
3½%
71%
Mariana Trench

Answers: 1—tide; 2—waves; 3—moon, sun; 4—currents; 5—prevailing winds; 6—density; 7—sodium chloride; 8—pressure; 9—salinity; 10—sediment; 11—trenches; 12—continental shelf

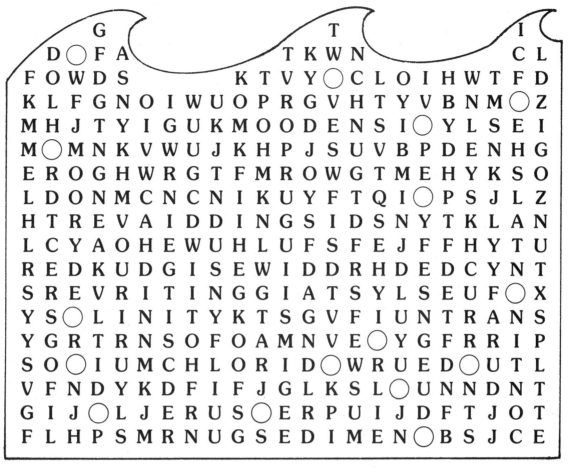

1. The slow, periodic rise and fall of water in the ocean is called the _____.

2. _____ transfer energy from one part of the ocean to another. Wind, earthquakes, and volcanic eruptions can cause them.

3. Tides are caused by the gravitational attraction between the Earth and the _____ and the Earth and the _____.

4. _____ in the ocean may be caused by wind or by density differences of ocean water. They are sometimes called "rivers" of the ocean.

5. Currents at the surface of the ocean are caused mostly by _____.

6. Deep-ocean currents are caused by differences in the _____ of the water.

7. Most of the salt in the sea is the same as ordinary table salt. This salt is called

_____.

8. The tremendous _____ deep in the ocean is created by the weight of water.

9. The total amount of dissolved solids in water is called _____. Almost all of the dissolved solids in seawater are salts.

10. In some areas, the ocean floor is covered by a thick layer of _____, which is made up of the remains of dead plants and animals, as well as other material.

11. The deepest points on the surface of the Earth are found in _____ in the ocean.

12. The gently sloping edge of a continent is called the _____.

CURRENTS WAVES CONTINENTAL SHELF DENSITY TRENCHES CONTINENTAL RISE
SALTS SALINITY SODIUM CHLORIDE PREVAILING WINDS OXYGEN VELOCITY PRESSURE
UPWELLINGS BREAKERS MID-OCEAN RIDGES TIDE MARS MOON SUN SEDIMENT SAND

LIFE IN THE OCEAN

I f you look at the ocean from the shore or from the deck of a boat, it's easy to think of it as one huge, unvarying mass of blue, salty water. But take a "deeper" look at the ocean, and you'll find that it's really very different in different places. Near the surface, the ocean is a sunlit world that changes from day to night and, in some parts of the world, from season to season. Dive deeper, and the ocean becomes cold, dim, and unchanging. And thousands of feet below the surface, the ocean is a region of near-freezing temperatures, crushing pressure, and complete darkness.

THE OCEAN, FROM TOP TO BOTTOM

Seaweeds, sea snakes, whales, whelks, penguins, porpoises, tuna, and tunicates are just a few of the many organisms that live in the ocean. Most marine plants and animals are adapted to living in one of three regions—the sunlight, twilight, or midnight zone. These zones are defined by the presence (or absence) of light. And they differ from one another in temperature, amount of pressure, and nutrient supply. (Instead of sunlight, twilight, and midnight zone, some marine scientists use the terms *surface waters, mid-waters,* and *deep sea* to describe the different regions in the ocean. And other scientists prefer to divide the ocean into two parts—a light and dark region.) Here's a look at each light zone and some of the plants and animals that live in them:

LIFE AT THE TOP

Sunlight on the Surface: Light streams through the "sunlight zone," the top layer of the ocean. This is the ocean's greenhouse, the only zone where there's enough light to support plant life. On the average, the sunlight zone ends at about 300 feet. But this lower boundary varies from just a few feet to more than 600 feet, depending on the part of the world and even the time of year. Although the sunlight zone makes up only a small part of the ocean (see diagram on page 18), more than 90 percent of all known marine species live here.

Drifters and Swimmers: Many animals in the sunlight zone get around either by drifting or swimming. The drifters include jellyfish, young crabs and fish, and microscopic plants and animals. These organisms, collectively called *plankton,* move along with the winds and currents. Some plankton have a limited swimming ability and can migrate daily in a vertical direction.

Dolphins, swordfish, sea turtles, and other swimmers make their own way through the ocean. Many have muscular, streamlined bodies that help them move through the water.

Precious Plankton: Planktonic organisms provide the basic source of food in the surface waters. Millions of microscopic *phytoplankton* (plant plankton) grow near the surface, bathed in sunlight and nourished by nutrients such as oxygen, carbon, nitrogen, and phosphorus from the surrounding water. Slightly larger *zooplankton* (animal plankton) feed on phytoplankton or on each other. In turn, animals such as fish, jellyfish, and even whales eat zooplankton. And many plankton-eating animals are preyed on by seabirds, seals, sharks, and other meat eaters. (For more about what marine animals eat and the importance of plankton, see "A Web on the Wall" on page 26.)

A Changing Place: Daily changes in sunlight affect organisms that live in the upper waters. For example, some kinds of fish remain far below the surface during the bright, sunlit hours, then feed closer to the surface at night when darkness helps hide them from predators. Seasonal variations in sunlight also affect some plants and animals. In temperate and polar regions, surface waters warm up in the spring and help stimulate explosive plankton growth. Some animals, such as gray whales, make seasonal migrations to gorge themselves in these plankton-rich areas.

Life from Death: When they die, inhabitants of the sunlight zone become food for animals that live deeper in the ocean. Dead plants and animals sink toward the ocean floor, gradually decomposing along the way and releasing precious nutrients that had been locked away in their body tissues. Some remains of dead plants and animals fall into deeper waters, where a variety of animals may feed on them. Even wastes from animals in the surface waters provide nutrients for organisms that live in the deep sea.

A Continental Close-Up: Life is most abundant in one special part of the sunlight zone—the waters over the continental shelves. In many parts of the world, these shallow waters harbor rich populations of plankton, fish, mammals, and birds. (In fact, more than half of the world's commercial fish catch comes from these waters.) And the shelf floor itself teems with animals that crawl on, burrow through, swim near, or stick to the bottom.

The abundance of nutrients in the sunlit continental waters promotes this amazing productivity. In some parts of the world, nutrients are brought to the shelf waters by *upwellings,* waters that move up the continental slope from deep in the ocean. Nutrients from the decomposing remains of dead plants and animals are also scooped off the shelf floor itself and carried closer to the surface by water that the wind has stirred up.

INTO THE MURKY MID-WATERS

Deeper and Dimmer: With increasing depth, the water pressure increases, the temperature drops sharply, and the light gradually dims. The next layer of the ocean, the "twilight zone," extends from the lower boundary of the sunlight zone down to about 3000 feet. Most of the sunlight has been absorbed by the upper layers of water, leaving the twilight zone cast in dim, blue light that barely forms silhouettes.

For Animals Only: Plants can't grow in these dimly lit mid-waters. Limited by a "plantless" food supply, the animals in this zone are smaller and less abundant than animals that live closer to the surface. Some twilight-zone dwellers, such as lantern fish and mid-water zooplankton, swim up into the sunlight zone each night to feed on the more plentiful food there. Others, such as hatchet fish, prey on animals within the twilight zone. And many twilight-zone animals survive by eating large pieces of animal and plant remains that drift down from the sunlight zone.

Lights On: *Bioluminescence,* the production of light by living creatures, is another common characteristic of organisms in the twilight waters. Many mid-water shrimp, squid, fish, and other animals have special light-producing organs on their bodies. Scientists think these lights may attract prey, identify potential mates, or surprise predators. (For more about "glow-in-the-dark" animals, see "Mysteries of the Deep" on page 24.) *(continued next page)*

THE DARK DEEP SEA

Life in the Pits: Beginning at about 3000 feet and stretching to the ocean floor, the "midnight zone" makes up about three-quarters of the total ocean. That's an estimated 250 million cubic miles of water!

Life isn't easy in the ocean's "basement." The water pressure here may exceed two tons per square inch, the temperature hovers near freezing, and it's completely dark. And these harsh conditions remain the same throughout the day and year. Scientists estimate that only one percent of all ocean species live in this zone.

Stunted and Slow: If you looked at a close-up photo of a fangtooth, angler fish, or other deep-sea predator, you'd probably be startled by its gaping mouth and sharp teeth. But, like many deep-sea animals, these fierce-looking predators are only a few inches long. In addition to being small, most deep-sea animals have a very low metabolic rate, which means that their digestive rate, heart rate, and other body functions are very slow compared to those of most other marine animals. Because of this, midnight-zone animals tend to grow very slowly and live for a long time.

Super Scavengers: Animal remains from the ocean's upper layers are a major source of food in the midnight zone. Chunks of flesh from the carcasses of whales and other large animals are quickly seized by active scavengers such as rattail fish, hagfish, sleeper sharks, and an occasional deep-sea octopus. Crabs, snails, shrimp, and smaller scavengers feed on the scraps left by larger animals. (For more about animals that live in the deep sea, see "Mysteries of the Deep" on page 24.)

On the Floor: The flat, largely featureless *abyssal plains* stretch across much of the deep-sea floor. Deep layers of silt called "ooze," formed over thousands of years by a steady rain of plankton remains, cover the plains. For the most part, the deep-sea floor is a pretty deserted place. That's because there's not a lot of food that far down. Some floor-dwelling animals, such as sea pens, are anchored in the ooze and filter tiny food particles from the surrounding water. Others, such as sea cucumbers and acorn worms, crawl along or burrow into the floor in their search for nutrients.

Hot Spots: Special vent communities found along deep-sea ridges are the exception to almost *every* generalization about the midnight zone. For one thing, a great number of animals live in a small area in these communities. They grow quickly and can become relatively large. And, unlike most other inhabitants of the deep-sea floor, these creatures don't depend on plant and animal remains from the surface waters (and ultimately, sunlight) for food.

These special deep-sea communities are clustered around *hydrothermal vents*—cracks in the Earth's crust that spew out hot, mineral-rich water. Special *chemosynthetic* bacteria use hydrogen sulfide that pours from the vents for energy to make food—in much the same way that green plants use sunlight in photosynthesis. All of the other animals living around the vents depend on these bacteria for food. Anemones, for example, filter the bacteria from the water. Others, such as eight-foot-long tube worms and foot-wide clams, have formed a special partnership with the bacteria. In place of a "gut," the worms and clams have masses of bacteria inside their body tissues that provide them with nutrients.

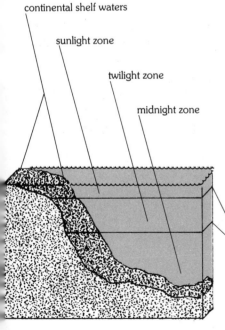

continental shelf waters

sunlight zone

twilight zone

midnight zone

300 ft
3000 ft

Alien Adventure

Listen to a story about life in the ocean.

Objectives:
Name and describe some of the creatures that live in the ocean.

Ages:
Primary and Intermediate

Materials:
- *copies of page 33*
- *pencils*
- *story on page 20*

Subjects:
Science and Language Arts

Your kids can get a feeling for the diversity of life in the ocean by listening to a short science fiction story. Begin by passing out copies of page 33. Then explain that you'll be reading a story about two children, Sarah and Abrahm, who travel to a strange and exciting place. (Don't tell the kids yet that the place Sarah and Abrahm travel to is the ocean.)

Explain that, on their journey, Abrahm and Sarah encounter many strange and interesting forms of life. What they see is represented by the pictures on page 33. When you get to a part in the story that describes one of the organisms that lives in this different world, the kids should look for the picture that fits the description and mark a number on it. For example, the first description in the story focuses on a creature that's "made up of dozens of long, thin stalks" that "seem to have little round tips." The kids should look for the picture that they think fits this description and mark a "1" in the blank. For the next description the kids should write a "2" on the picture they choose, and so on up to "8." (Tell the kids not to worry about the letter printed in each picture. You'll be using these letters later to go over the answers.)

To make it easier for younger kids, you might want to stop reading after each description and give them some time to search before getting on with the story. You might also want to read the story twice. The first time through the kids can simply listen, and the second time through they can look for the matching pictures.

In the story, the name of each creature being described is printed in bold type in parentheses—but don't read these names to the kids. (You'll need to know the names later when you go over the answers.) When you finish reading "Journey to Another World," tell the kids that the different world Abrahm and Sarah "visited" really exists—right here on Earth. Ask if anyone has any idea what that place is. Then explain that the kinds of life described in the story represent just a few of the unusual species that live in the world's oceans. All of the species in the story live in the Atlantic Ocean.

Before going over which picture fits which description, you might want to have the kids sort the pictures according to which ones they think may be plants and which ones they think may be animals by writing a "P" or an "A" on each picture. When they've finished, explain that *all* of the pictures are of animals. Unlike plants, none of the creatures we've pictured can get its energy by making its own food. Instead, these organisms get their energy by eating other animals, plants, or both. (The pink-tipped anemone is a special case: Tiny algae often live in its cells, and the anemone uses some of the food energy the algae produce.) Explain that in the ocean—more than in any other habitat on Earth—it's difficult to tell just by looking at them whether some organisms are plants or animals.

Now go over the correct order of the pictures using the numbered pictures below and the descriptions listed under "Incredible Creatures" on page 21. (The letter in parentheses after the name of each organism indicates which picture is which on the Copycat Page.) Also use the descriptions to talk about each organism.

(continued next page)

1. pink-tipped sea anemone

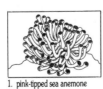
2. magnificent feather duster worm

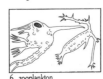
3. tube sponge

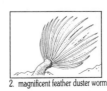
4. rough file shell

5. Atlantic long-fin squid

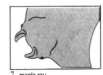
6. zooplankton

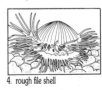
7. manta ray

8. gulper eel

Sarah and Abrahm were on board a very special ship, traveling through a strange and wonderful world. There were so many new sights to see! Sarah set the ship's controls on slow cruise, then settled in front of a big window.

"Look at *that*!" Abrahm shouted, pointing at something out the window.

Sarah pulled the ship in close to a funny-looking object that was attached to a rock. It looked like it was made up of dozens of long, skinny stalks. The stalks, which were swaying gently back and forth, all seemed to have little round tips. **(pink-tipped sea anemone)**

The ship drifted to one side and something else caught Sarah's eye.

"Wow—look at that long tube with all those feathery things coming out of the end," she said. **(magnificent feather duster worm)**

Abrahm laughed. "It looks like a mini feather duster!"

As the ship moved on through an area of rough, rocky hills, Sarah and Abrahm saw other amazing sights. They weren't sure if some of the things they were looking at were plants or animals! In one area they saw a group of odd-looking tubes of different lengths poking up from the rocks. **(tube sponge)** On a rocky ledge in another area they found something that looked sort of like a clam with lots of long, thin things coming out of its shell. **(rough file shell)**

Eventually the kids found themselves traveling over a wide, rocky slope. They stopped the ship, and after a while a very strange creature drifted up to one side of the window. Its body was beyond the window's edge, so all the kids could see was its face.

"Now *that's* weird," said Sarah, moving closer to the window. Abrahm agreed. The creature just hung there, its big, unblinking eye staring back at the kids. Several long, fleshy limbs hung down from its head. **(Atlantic long-fin squid)** As the creature moved away, Sarah wondered if the fleshy limbs were arms or legs.

"Hey," Abrahm said suddenly, "we forgot about the Scannerscope."

The Scannerscope could take pictures of tiny things outside the ship, then show them magnified on a big screen. Below the pictures, the Scannerscope printed a paragraph that told about the pictures it was showing.

Abrahm turned on the Scannerscope, and right away dozens of funny-looking "monsters" appeared on the screen. One had a pair of antennae that looked a little like tree branches, and the other had a big eye and a long, pointed limb that looked like a horn. **(zooplankton)**

Sarah read the description beneath the picture. "Just think," she said. "There are *billions* of those little things out there. But most of them are too tiny for us to get a good look at with our bare eyes."

"Well, *that's* not too tiny for us to see!" said Abrahm, pointing to a huge, dark creature that was moving toward the window. It had a small eye on either side of its head and a very strange-looking mouth. Slowly flapping its "wings," the creature turned and glided gracefully past the ship. **(manta ray)**

There was a canyon up ahead, and the kids decided to explore. The light got dimmer and dimmer as they guided the ship down, down, down into the canyon. Pretty soon it was as dark as night. But around the ship in the darkness the kids could see tiny lights swirling around.

The ship's automatic headlights flicked on and Sarah and Abrahm suddenly saw creatures darting around where the lights had been before. One of the creatures was almost too strange to believe. Its body was long and skinny, but its head was huge! The creature moved past the ship with its big mouth wide open. As it passed the window, it seemed to look at the kids with one of its beady eyes. **(gulper eel)**

"Wow," said Abrahm, watching the creature as it disappeared into the distance. "That was the neatest thing we've seen yet!"

"It sure was," Sarah agreed. She turned the ship around and started the long journey home. "But," she added, "who knows what we'll see on the way back?"

INCREDIBLE CREATURES

Pink-tipped sea anemone (1—H)
- Anemones, relatives of corals and jellyfish, look more like plants than animals. In fact, they're named after the wild-flowers known as anemones.
- An anemone usually has dozens of tentacles. The tentacles, which surround the animal's mouth, have stinging capsules that can paralyze small animals that swim within range. The anemone uses its tentacles to pull its prey into its mouth.
- Anemones often attach themselves to firm surfaces such as rocks. They usually stay put, although they can slowly move to another area.

Magnificent feather duster worm (2—C)
- Feather dusters are fanworms that build their own tube-shaped "houses." They make the tubes out of mud, sand, pebbles, and/or other materials found on the sea floor.
- Magnificent feather dusters and many other fanworms attach one end of their tube to a rock or other surface. Their feathery "fans" come out of the free end of the tube and surround the mouth.
- A fanworm's "fans" filter tiny particles from the water and transport them down into the animal's mouth.

Tube sponge (3—A)
- All kinds of interesting shapes characterize the sponges. Some look like blobs, some are round, and others are vase-shaped. And a few, such as tube sponges, are tubular.
- Water flows into pores on a sponge's surface, bringing with it tiny particles and bacteria that the sponge eats. Water then flows out through the large openings in the sponge, carrying wastes with it.
- Tube sponges often attach themselves to dead coral.

Rough file shell (4—E)
- When file shells need to make a quick getaway, they swim by jet propulsion, rapidly clapping their shells together.
- A file shell's many tentacles help it sense its environment.
- File shells are filter feeders. They bring water into their shells and filter out tiny organisms and particles from the water.

Atlantic long-fin squid (5—F)
- The Atlantic long-fin squid, about a foot and a half in length, is an average-sized squid.
- Squid can pull water into their gill chamber through slits behind their head, then push it out forcefully through a special siphon. This "jet action" helps them move quickly through the water.
- Squid have two tentacles and eight shorter arms, all of which have suckers on them.
- Squid squirt out an inky substance when attacked. This "ink" serves to confuse enemies while the squid escapes.

Zooplankton (6—D)
- Plankton are drifting organisms that live in the ocean and other bodies of water. Many types of plankton are microscopic.
- There are two basic kinds of plankton: *phytoplankton* (plant plankton) and *zooplankton* (animal plankton). The plankton described in the story are zooplankton.
- Plankton drift along in the water, going wherever the currents take them. A few kinds of plankton can swim, but none are strong enough to overcome waves and currents.
- Plankton are an important source of food for many kinds of sea animals.

Manta ray (7—G)
- Many kinds of rays live near the ocean floor. But the manta ray lives near the surface. Here it can take advantage of plentiful supplies of plankton, its main food.
- Manta rays and many other kinds of rays "fly" through the water, flapping their broad, flat fins. Mantas feed as they "fly" by keeping their huge mouth open and letting the plankton-laden water flow across special filters in their mouth.
- Mantas are the largest of the rays. From fin tip to fin tip, they can be more than 20 feet wide.

Gulper eel (8—B)
- Some scientists think gulper eels catch small animals to eat by swimming with their mouth open.
- Gulpers live deep in the ocean, where there's little or no light. (You might want to point out that many of the animals that live in dark waters, including gulpers, have luminescent patches or spots on their bodies. In the story, Abrahm and Sarah saw the glowing, flashing lights that some of these deep-sea animals produce.)

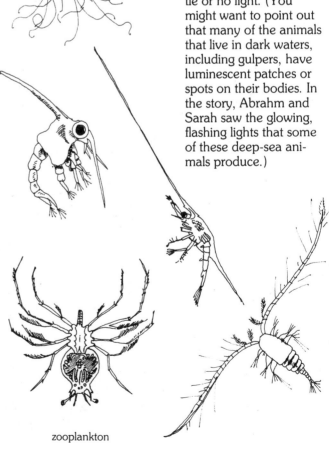

zooplankton

Ocean Odyssey

Explore the diversity of marine life by visiting an aquarium.

Objective:
Describe several marine animals and plants.

Ages:
Primary, Intermediate, and Advanced

Materials:
- *pictures of marine plants and animals*
Primary
- *construction paper*
- *scissors*
- *yarn*
- *paper punch*
Intermediate and Advanced
- *clipboards*
- *pencils*
- *copies of scavenger hunt clues on page 23*
- *mural paper (optional)*
- *paint, crayons, or markers (optional)*

Subject:
Science

Most kids have been to a zoo, but a lot of kids have never visited an aquarium. Aquariums are showcases of aquatic life—and they're great places to visit on a field trip. Here are some ideas that can help your group get the most out of a trip to an aquarium.

BEFORE YOU GO

Visit the aquarium yourself sometime before the trip so you can adapt the activity to the exhibits. You should also contact the education department of the aquarium to schedule a time and date for your visit. (Remember that April, May, and June are often an aquarium's busiest months.) Ask if they offer any educational materials, and discuss coordinating your activity with any educational programs the aquarium might provide. And if you have a large group, keep in mind that you'll need to take some extra adults on the trip. (Most aquariums prefer that kids tour the exhibits in small groups accompanied by adults.)

You should also introduce the kids to the diversity of ocean life before visiting the aquarium. Show them pictures of different marine plants and animals as you discuss some or all of the topics listed below. (See pages 16–18 for more information.)

TOPICS TO TOUCH ON
- where plants and animals live in the ocean (in shallow water, in deep water, on the bottom, near the surface, in the mid-waters)
- ocean habitats (coral reefs, kelp forests, and so on)
- how ocean animals move
- how ocean animals get their food
- how ocean animals protect themselves from predators
- marine creatures that live together in special relationships (see "Reef Buddies" on page 41)
- body shapes of ocean creatures
- marine animals that produce their own light

Monterey Bay Aquarium

FOR YOUNGER KIDS: SEARCHING FOR SHAPES

Before your trip, cut a variety of generalized sea plants and animals out of construction paper. (See the silhouettes in the margin for ideas. The bibliography on page 67 has a listing of books with good pictures.) You'll need one shape for every child in your group. Then punch a hole at the top of each shape and thread a piece of yarn through it so each child can wear one around his or her neck.

When you get to the aquarium, give each child a shape. Tell the kids that they'll be looking for a plant or animal that resembles the shape they're wearing. At each display ask the kids if they can find a living thing that matches their shape. Then talk about some of the plants or animals.

(You can be as general or as specific as you want to be. For example, if you know something about any of the organisms in a particular display, you can point out some interesting facts about it. Or you can just focus on colors, patterns, the organism's behavior, and so on.) You can also have the kids look for some of the scavenger hunt clues listed at the end of the activity. And you might want to have them try to find things that match the color of their paper shape.

After the trip, review the diversity of marine life. You might also want to encourage the kids to act out the behavior of some of the animals they saw.

FOR OLDER KIDS: A SCAVENGER HUNT

Before your trip, modify the scavenger hunt list below to fit the level of your group. Make enough copies for everyone. When you get to the aquarium, give each person a pencil, a copy of the list, and a clipboard. Tell the kids that their goal is to find an animal or plant that fits each clue on the list. They should base their answers on the appearance of the organisms that they see and on any written information at

the displays. They can write the name of the plant or animal next to the clue it fits, and/or they can sketch it on the back of their paper.

After the trip, go over the results of the scavenger hunt as a group. And as a follow-up, you may want to have the kids make a mural showing the variety of life they saw at the aquarium.

SCAVENGER HUNT CLUES

As you walk through the aquarium, try to find:

1. an animal that blends into its surroundings
2. a species of fish in which the male and female are different colors
3. an animal that can change colors
4. a very flat fish
5. an animal that produces light
6. an animal that lives in a shell
7. an animal that's attached to something else
8. an animal that eats other animals
9. an animal that looks like a plant
10. an animal that spends most of its time on the bottom of the ocean
11. a type of seaweed
12. an animal that escapes enemies by swimming very quickly
13. an animal or plant that drifts near the surface
14. an animal that must go to the surface to breathe air
15. an animal with tentacles
16. an animal that spends part of its time in water and part of its time on land
17. a brightly colored animal
18. an animal or plant that lives on the shore
19. an animal that's bigger than you are
20. an animal that's smaller than an apple
21. an animal that escapes enemies by hiding in the sand
22. an animal that escapes enemies by hiding between rocks
23. a fish that swims in a school
24. a plant that's attached to the bottom
25. an animal with more than two eyes

Mysteries of the Deep

Act out a poem about the ocean's depths and make an ocean flip-up.

Objectives:
Describe conditions in the ocean's depths. Talk about how animals that live in these regions are adapted to their habitats.

Ages:
Primary and Intermediate

Materials:
- *copies of page 34*
- *scissors*
- *pictures of luminescent deep-sea creatures*
- *staplers or tape*

Subject:
Science

Imagine you're in the cold, dim depths of the ocean. Here and there you can see small lights dancing eerily. If you could somehow switch on a floodlight, you might discover the source of the dancing lights. For example, you might see some small but monstrous-looking fish swimming nearby. Many fish that live in the ocean's depths have built-in "flashlights" in the form of light-producing organs or luminescent patches of skin.

Being able to light up is just one adaptation that helps some animals survive in the dark depths of the ocean. To help your kids learn more about the deep sea and the creatures that live there, try the following activity. But before you start, make enough copies of page 34 for everyone. Then cut each page apart along the dashed line and put the two halves aside.

Begin by using the information under "Way Down Below" on the next page to talk about the ocean's depths. Don't talk about bioluminescence yet, though. The kids will learn about marine animals that light up by looking at their Copycat Page.

Next pass out a copy of the dark half of page 34 to each person. As the kids look at the picture, tell them to imagine that they've taken a trip way down into the depths of the ocean. The sea around them is dark. But as they look out the window of

their *submersible* (a submersible is a small submarine specially built for scientific research), they can see tiny, moving lights that look like the light-colored shapes in the scene they're looking at.

Ask the kids what they think the light-colored shapes are, then pass out the light half of page 34. Tell the kids that their submersible is equipped with a big floodlight that can light up the area around them. When they switch on the floodlight, they see a scene out the window similar to the one shown on the light half of the page. And they discover that the darting lights belong to deep-sea creatures. (Explain that it's not likely that they'd see all of the organisms we've pictured at any one time. For example, some animals tend to stick to very deep areas within the ocean, in the midnight zone, and some spend more time higher up, in the twilight zone. [For more about these zones, see pages 16–18.] We've pictured all of the animals together to show the kids several of the different kinds of animals that live in deep waters. Also, the creatures aren't drawn to scale. For example the gulper eel, which is about two and a half feet long, is much larger than the other creatures, most of which are only a couple of inches long!)

While the kids are looking at the two parts of the Copycat Page, discuss bioluminescence, using the information in "Turn on the Lights!" During your discussion, show the kids pictures of luminescent creatures. A good source of pictures is "Lights on for Lunch" on pages 41–47 of the January, 1984 issue of *Ranger Rick*. Then have the kids perform "Down in the Deep" (on the next page) by repeating each line of the poem after you and acting out the motions.

To wrap up the activity, have the kids tape or staple the dark half of the Copycat Page on top of the light half. They can look at the dark half for an idea of what the ocean's depths look like—then flip up the page to see what the scene might look like if the kids could somehow light it up.

angler fish

DOWN IN THE DEEP
Down in the deep, within the sea—
That's not the place for you and me!

Shake head "no";
point to others and
then to yourself.

'Cause way down there, so I've been
told,
It's dark as night and freezing cold.

Cover eyes with
hands, then hug your-
self as if cold.

But in this place, down in the deep,
Strange creatures swim and crawl
and creep.

Make swimming or
crawling motions with
hands.

And tiny monsters blink and glow,
Down in the deep, way down below.

Bare teeth like a
monster.

WAY DOWN BELOW

Slim Pickin's: Because of the darkness in most deep waters, plants can't grow. (Plants need sunlight for photosynthesis.) This dearth of plants sets deep-sea communities apart from most other natural communities.

In most habitats, plants—either directly or indirectly—provide food for all the animals that live there. Some animals eat the plants, and others eat the animals that eat the plants. Because there are no plants in the ocean's deepest reaches, the food supply is scarce.

Making the Most of It: Some deep-sea animals eat the bacteria-rich ooze on the ocean's floor. And some prey on other deep-sea animals. In fact, some predatory fish that live in the ocean's depths, such as the gulper eel on the Copycat Page, even eat animals that are as big as or bigger than they are! These fish have special expandable stomachs that can stretch to hold a really big meal. Being able to eat a huge meal at one time is an advantage in a habitat where meals are few and far between.

Turn on the Lights!: The deeper you go in the ocean, the darker it gets. (In general, sunlight can penetrate the ocean to a depth of only about 600 feet.) Organisms in these dark waters have adapted in a number of ways. As we mentioned in the introduction, for example, many fish and other organisms that live in dark waters can glow. These luminescent creatures use their "flashlights" for different purposes. Some flash their lights on and off, which helps them attract a mate. Others, such as the angler fish on the Copycat Page, lure prey within striking distance with special glowing appendages that look like worms or other food. And some startle predators with their luminescent abilities.

Many luminescent fish look like strange, glowing monsters. But point out to the kids that most of these "monsters" are very small—no bigger than a couple of inches long!

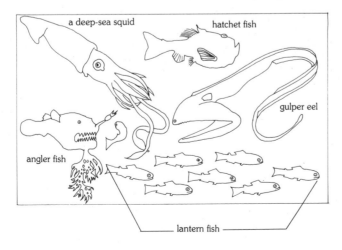

a deep-sea squid   hatchet fish

gulper eel

angler fish

lantern fish

A Web on the Wall

Objectives:
Name some marine animals and describe what they eat. Define food chain and food web. Explain the importance of phytoplankton in marine food webs.

Ages:
Intermediate and Advanced

Materials:
- *bulletin board*
- *pictures of plankton*
- *chalkboard or easel paper*
- *construction paper*
- *scissors*
- *small bags*
- *tape*
- *glue*
- *staplers or tacks*
- *markers or crayons*
- *reference books*
- *paper plates*
- *paper*
- *cotton or tissue paper (optional)*
- *pantyhose*
- *clear container*
- *needle and thread*
- *rubber band*
- *hand lenses and microscopes*
- *wire*

Subjects:
Science and Art

people
↑
cattle
↑
plants

Either directly or indirectly, almost every animal in the ocean depends on microscopic phytoplankton for food. By making a three-dimensional bulletin board, your kids can see that phytoplankton is important to many kinds of animals, from scallops to whales.

Before you begin, copy each of the names in bold from the information under "Members of the Web" on page 28 on separate slips of paper and put the slips in a bag. Then, on construction paper, copy and enlarge each of the outlines pictured near the names of the different marine animals. (The number beside each name indicates the number of copies of each outline to make.) You should make each outline at least a few inches long and use different-colored paper for similar outlines, such as the anchovy and mackerel. Then put the outlines for each creature in a separate bag and label each bag.

Start the activity by discussing the concept of *food chains*. Ask the kids to raise their hands if they had a hamburger, steak, or some other kind of beef for dinner last night. Write "people" on a chalkboard or sheet of easel paper, then ask the kids if they know what animal beef comes from. Add the word "cattle" below "people," then ask what cattle eat. Add the word "plants" below "cattle," then draw arrows between the three words (see diagram). Explain that you've just drawn a simple food chain. A food chain shows the transfer of energy, in the form of food, from one organism to another.

Explain that plants form the base of almost every food chain on Earth. Plants use energy from the sun to make their own food through photosynthesis. In turn, some animals eat plants, and other animals eat the plant-eating animals.

Now tell the kids that, like animals on land, most animals that live in the ocean depend on plants for food. And the most important marine plants are *phytoplankton*. Show the kids pictures of different kinds of phytoplankton and explain that millions of these tiny plants drift near the ocean's surface. Tiny animals called *zooplankton* eat the phytoplankton, and so do clams, corals, and small fish. (Show the kids pictures of zooplankton.) Ask the kids if they can guess what kinds of animals eat zooplankton. (some fish, jellyfish, and even some kinds of whales) Then explain that many larger fish and other animals eat the animals that feed on zooplankton.

Next explain to the kids that they'll be learning more about marine organisms. Divide the group into 12 teams and have each team pick one of the slips of paper you made earlier. Explain that all of these organisms are found in the Pacific Ocean off the coast of Washington. Each team will be doing some research to answer these questions about their organism:
- What does it look like?
- About what size is it?
- Where does it live in the ocean—near the surface, on the bottom, or in the mid-waters?
- What does it eat, and how does it get its food?

Give the kids reference books and time to answer the questions. If the kids have trouble finding a specific animal or plant, such as "giant Pacific octopus," have them look for general information under the heading of "octopus." (See the bibliography on page 67 for reference book suggestions.)

When everyone has finished the research, tell the kids they'll be making a three-dimensional bulletin board that shows all of their organisms and what they eat. Explain that each team will make at least one three-dimensional figure of their animal or plant. They can make the whole body of some animals such as the scallop or octopus and just the head and mouth of the others. See "Building the Bulletin Board" on the page 28 for how to make a construction-paper mouth that can be adapted to represent most of these animals, along with some other helpful hints. (Since there are so many types of plankton, have the plankton teams use the simple outlines that you enlarged to make their figures.)

Now pass out construction paper, scis-

Wendy Silverman

sors, glue, and markers or crayons, and let the kids start making their figures. Teams that finish early can cover the bulletin board with a background of green or blue construction paper and add a brown ocean floor.

As the teams finish, have them staple or tack their animals to the bulletin board. (See "Building the Bulletin Board.") The photo above shows one way to put together the bulletin board. You can adapt your board to fit the level of your group.

Then, starting with the phytoplankton group, have each team explain what their creature needs to survive. (For example, phytoplankton need sunlight and nutrients.) You can check their answers against the information under "Members of the Web." Also have the kids check the other creatures on the board to see if their animal eats any of them. If so, the kids should take one or more of the outlines from the bags you filled earlier and tape them inside their animal's mouth or on the body part

that captures food. For example, the octopus team could tape a scallop to one of the octopus' arms. Then the kids should draw a line from their animal to the animal it eats—in this case from the octopus to the scallop.

When the bulletin board is finished, ask the kids the following questions. (To give the kids more time to think, you may want to have them write down their answers, then discuss them as a group.)

● How is the finished board different from the simple food chain you drew on the board earlier? (It includes many food chains and is more complex.)

● Which animals would probably have trouble surviving if there were no more anchovies or phytoplankton? (If there were no anchovies, all of the organisms except the scallop and plankton would have trouble. And if phytoplankton disappeared, all of the animals would have trouble.)

Explain that the bulletin board shows a *food web*—a series of interconnecting food chains. A food web is a more realistic way of explaining the transfer of energy between animals and plants than a food chain because most animals tend to eat more than one kind of food. Be sure to point out that plants (in this case, phytoplankton) almost always form the base of a food web. You can show that even a top predator such as the killer whale depends on these small plants by tracing the connecting lines from the killer whale back to the phytoplankton.

(continued next page)

A PHYTOPLANKTON FIELD TRIP

After learning about the importance of phytoplankton and zooplankton in marine food webs, your kids can take a close-up look at plankton. If you live near the coast, take the kids on a field trip to the beach or to a salt marsh to collect water samples. (If you live inland, try a freshwater pond.) You can cut off one leg of a pair of pantyhose to make a plankton net. First cut off the foot and sew the larger end to a circle of wire. Then put the smaller end over the top of a clear container

and secure it with a rubber band (see diagram). As you swish the net through the water, the pantyhose will funnel plankton into the container. Use hand lenses and microscopes to look at the plankton you collect. Also see *Pond Life* by Dr. George K. Reid (Golden Press, 1967) and *The Water Naturalist* by Heather Angel and Pat Wolsely (Facts on File, 1982) for more tips on collecting plankton and drawings to help you identify different kinds of plankton.

BUILDING THE BULLETIN BOARD

Most of the animals' mouths can be made out of construction paper. Here's how:

1. Fold a piece of construction paper in half. (The size of the paper will vary, depending on how big a mouth you're making.)
2. Make a perpendicular cut on the folded side of the paper, about midway between either end.
3. Fold back one side of the cut to make a triangle (see diagram). Strongly crease the fold. Repeat with other side of the cut.

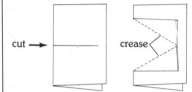

cut →   crease

fold paper back, away from slit

4. Unfold both triangles, bend them back the other way, and crease them again.

5. Unfold the paper and push the folds outward. Then bend the paper slightly to open and close the mouth (see diagram).
6. Depending on the animal, you may want to glue the mouth to a larger piece of paper that's shaped to resemble the rest of the head or body. Or you can just add eyes, teeth, and other features around the mouth.

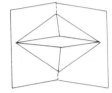

Here are some other tips:
- Make the jellyfish and scallop out of paper plates.
- Fringe paper to make the humpback whale's baleen.

- Make a lot of plankton figures to represent the abundance of these tiny plants and animals.
- Try to make the sizes of the figures in proportion to each other. For example, the whales and shark should be larger than the mackerel and anchovy.
- Place the creatures according to where they live in the ocean. For example, the octopus should be near the ocean floor and the anchovy should be near the surface.
- Make the figures as three-dimensional as possible. Some animals could be stuffed with cotton or tissue paper to make them stick out from the board.
- You may also want to make name tags for each animal on the bulletin board so they're easier to identify.

MEMBERS OF THE WEB

Phytoplankton (4)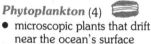
- microscopic plants that drift near the ocean's surface
- absorb sunlight and nutrients from water
- diatoms are one of the most common kinds of phytoplankton

Zooplankton (12)
- tiny animals that live near the ocean's surface and in deeper waters
- some kinds of zooplankton feed on phytoplankton; others feed on other zooplankton
- most are very small, though some, such as *krill,* grow to be several inches long
- some, such as *copepods,* have feathery body parts that help filter phytoplankton from the water

Rock scallop (2)
- a shellfish that lives on the ocean bottom
- largest living scallop—grows to be 4 to 11 inches long
- eats phytoplankton, along with other small particles of food

- filters food through its gills (gills are also used for breathing)

Northern anchovy (12)
- a small fish that usually stays near the ocean's surface
- about 9 inches long
- feeds mostly on zooplankton
- netlike parts of its gills strain zooplankton from water

Chub mackerel (4)
- swims near the ocean's surface and in deeper waters
- about 18 inches long
- feeds on krill (a kind of zooplankton), squid, and anchovies

Lion's mane jellyfish
- drifts near the ocean's surface
- one of the largest jellyfish in the world—most are 1 to 2 feet wide, but some may be 8 feet wide
- its stinging tentacles paralyze prey such as zooplankton and young fish

Giant Pacific octopus
- spends most of its time on the ocean bottom
- feeds on shrimp, crabs, scallops, abalones, and clams
- traps prey with its arms, then tears it with its sharp beak

Blue shark
- found near the ocean's surface and in deeper waters
- about 12 feet long
- feeds on squid and fish such as anchovies and mackerel

Northern fur seal (1)
- spends most of its time near the ocean's surface
- can grow to be 6 feet long
- may dive 300 feet in search of prey
- eats squid and small fish such as anchovies and herring

Humpback whale (1)
- found near the ocean's surface and to depths of about 130 feet
- about 53 feet long
- eats mostly krill and other types of zooplankton; sometimes eats anchovies and other small fish
- huge, brushlike baleen on upper jaw strain zooplankton from water

Killer whale (orca)
- usually found near the ocean's surface
- may be 31 feet long
- eats other whales (such as humpbacks), seals, and fish such as mackerel

Brandt's cormorant
- a seabird that nests on the coast and feeds in coastal waters
- dives into water to catch small fish such as herring and anchovies

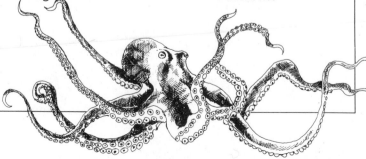

From Surface to Sea Floor

Make a pull-through that shows the different zones of life in the ocean.

Objectives:
Describe the three zones of life in the open ocean. Give an example of an animal that lives in each zone and explain how it is adapted to its habitat.

Ages:
Intermediate and Advanced

Materials:
- *copies of pages 32 and 35*
- *copy of cover on page 31*
- *construction paper*
- *glue*
- *scissors*
- *crayons or markers*
- *stapler*
- *tape*
- *paper*
- *pencils*
- *chalkboard or easel paper (optional)*
- *picture of a submersible such as Alvin (optional)*

Subjects:
Science and Language Arts

Traveling through the ocean depths in small submersibles, ocean explorers have been eye to eye with glowing hatchet fish, sharp-nosed swordfish, creeping sea cucumbers, and other ocean inhabitants. In the first part of this activity, your kids can make a pull-through that shows some of these creatures. And in the second part, they can use poetry to describe these animals and the different zones where they live.

Before you begin the activity, make a copy of page 31. Cut along the dashed line below the pull-through cover at the top of the page. Then place the cover in the center of an 8½ × 11″ piece of paper and make enough copies of it for your group.

PART 1: DIVING THROUGH THE ZONES

Begin by asking the kids to think about how the ocean's surface waters differ from the waters that are thousands of feet deeper. Using the background information on pages 16–18, talk about the kids' ideas and explain the differences between the sunlight, twilight, and midnight zones. (You may want to copy the diagram on page 18 onto a chalkboard or piece of easel paper.)

Next tell the kids that scientists are most familiar with the animals and plants that live in the sunlight zone, since these waters are close to the surface and relatively easy to study. But people know a lot less about life in the deeper parts of the ocean. Since the 1960s, scientists have traveled to these depths in submarinelike vehicles called *submersibles*. (You may want to show the kids a picture of a submersible such as *Alvin*.) Although they aren't very big (*Alvin* is 24 feet long and holds only three people), submersibles can withstand the intense pressure of the deep sea.

Next tell the kids that they'll be making a pull-through that will give them an idea of what a scientist might see on a submersible dive to the bottom of the Atlantic Ocean. Pass out copies of page 35, copies of the cover that you made earlier, construction paper, scissors, markers or crayons, and glue, and have the kids follow the directions below to make a pull-through.

MAKING THE PULL-THROUGH

THE INSIDE STRIP
1. Color the three different zones on page 35. (The twilight zone is cut in half.) Color the sunlight zone (to 300 feet) light blue, the twilight zone (to 3000 feet) dark blue, and the midnight zone (to bottom) black. Don't color the creatures!
2. Glue the Copycat Page onto a piece of construction paper. (Use a thin layer of glue and spread it evenly over the entire back of the paper.)
3. Cut along the dashed vertical lines so that you have two long strips. Cut off all of the excess construction paper, except for the paper at the top of the twilight zone. (Leaving extra construction paper at the top of the twilight zone will make the strip sturdier.)
4. Put the strips together so that the twilight zone is complete. Tape along both sides of the strip (see diagram on next page).

THE COVER
1. Cut out the circle on the pull-through cover. (It may be easier to first poke a hole in the center of the circle with a sharp pencil.) Also cut out the small box next to the circle.
2. Glue the cover to a piece of construction paper. Be sure to put a thin line of glue *only* along the vertical sides of the cover, leaving the bottom and top unglued (see diagram on next page).

(continued next page)

When the two parts are completed, have the kids insert the pull-through into the cover so that the top of the sunlight zone shows through the viewing port. (The depth and temperature window should be to the right of the viewing port.) Then, to help keep the pull-through "on line" as it moves through the cover, have the kids staple the cover together as shown in the diagram below.

Let the kids "descend" to the bottom a few times on their own. Point out that because some animals would be close to the submersible and others would be farther away, some appear larger than others. (Refer to information under "Who's Who in the Zones" on page 32 for actual sizes.) Also be sure to point out that the depth scale isn't in proportion for all three zones. To show the diversity of life throughout the ocean, we gave all the zones equal room on the pull-through. But the twilight and midnight zones are larger than the sunlight zone. You might also want to point out that the temperatures on the pull-through are average temperatures. In the ocean, water temperatures may vary depending on the season and location.

Next pass out copies of page 32. If you're working with younger kids, go over the information on the page as a group. Older kids can read the page on their own

to learn about each of the animals. (They can identify the animals by matching the numbers next to the animals' names with the figures in the margin.)

Have the kids color in all the animals on the pull-through according to the information on their sheets. Afterward ask the kids if they can make any generalizations about the characteristics of life in the different zones. (Animals in the twilight and midnight zones are generally smaller than those in the sunlight zone, and many animals in the twilight zone are luminescent. Many animals in the sunlight zone have dark backs and light bellies. When viewed from above this countershading helps them blend in with the darker waters below, and when viewed from below, it helps them blend in with the lighter waters above. See the background information on pages 16–18 for other generalizations.)

Also explain that although all these animals live in the Atlantic Ocean, it's unlikely that you'd find all of them in the same place at the same time. It's also unlikely that you'd see so many animals in the same small area, since life is widespread in the open ocean —especially in the twilight and midnight zones.

To finish up this part of the activity, the kids can decorate the pull-through cover to resemble what they think the inside of a submersible might look like.

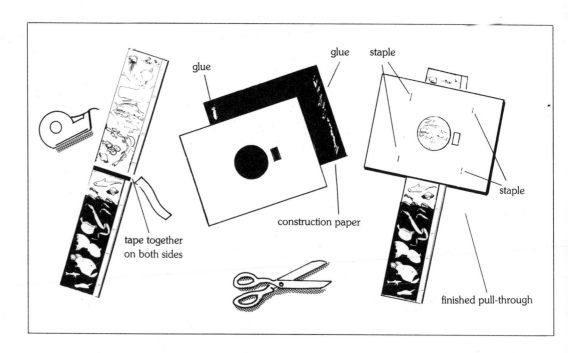

tape together on both sides

glue

glue   staple

construction paper

staple

finished pull-through

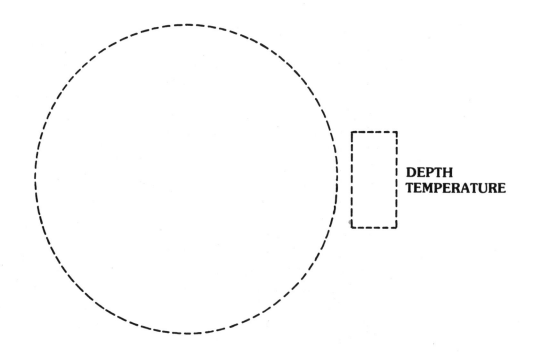

**DEPTH
TEMPERATURE**

PART 2: PICTURE POETRY

As a group, make a list of adjectives that describe the three zones of life and the creatures that live in them. Words such as *sunny, sparkling, black, dim, shadowy, murky,* and *crushing* could describe the zones. And *fast, speedy, strong, sharp-toothed, ugly, scary, floating, light-bearing,* and *big-mouthed* could describe some of the animals shown in the pull-through.

Tell the kids that these words help to create images of the different zones and the creatures that live in them. But these words can be even more descriptive if they're arranged to form a picture. Copy the example below on the board or easel

paper. Tell the kids that this form of poetry is called *picture poetry.* They'll be making up their own picture poems to describe the creatures and/or zones they learned about from the zone pull-through. Explain that they can use words from the list on the board, along with any other words they think of. Also explain that their poems don't have to rhyme and that they can use as few or as many words as they want to create a picture.

Pass out paper and pencils to the kids and give them time to make up some picture poems. Afterward, have volunteers share their poems with the rest of the group.

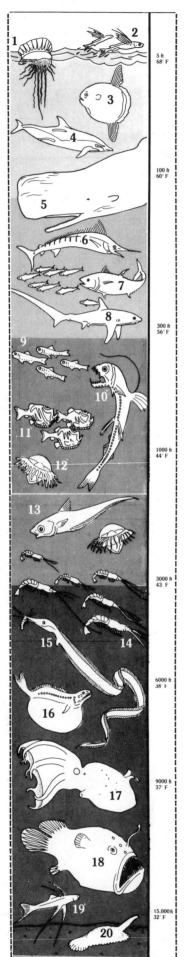

SUNLIGHT ZONE

1. Portuguese man-of-war
- purple body with long, purple and white tentacles
- tentacles may be over 100 feet long
- small fish are paralyzed by stinging tentacles, then eaten

2. Flying fish
- doesn't really fly—gains speed as it swims, then leaps from water and glides
- body is silver
- about 9 inches long

3. Ocean sunfish
- about 15 feet long and weighs more than a ton
- body is gray or brown
- eats jellyfish

4. Striped dolphin
- eats small fish and squid
- about 8 feet long
- back is dark blue and belly is white

5. Sperm whale
- about 56 feet long and weighs about 43 tons
- body is gray or black
- may eat a ton of food a day
- commonly dives to depths of more than 3000 feet in search of giant squid and other prey

6. Blue marlin
- about 12 feet long and weighs about 1000 pounds
- swipes its swordlike nose through schools of fish, then eats wounded ones
- back is blue and belly is white

7. Bluefin tuna
- usually swims in schools
- about 14 feet long and weighs about 1800 pounds
- back is blue-black, sides are silver-gray, and belly is white

8. Thresher shark
- about 16 feet long and weighs about 500 pounds
- back is olive-green or brown-gray and belly is white
- swims into schools of fish; stuns some fish by hitting them with its long tail, then eats them

TWILIGHT ZONE

9. Lantern fish
- 2 to 3 inches long
- swims closer to surface at night to feed on zooplankton
- body is pale brown or gray and speckled with many lights

10. Viperfish
- jaws can open wide to catch large prey
- about 8 to 10 inches long
- body is dark brown or black
- single line of lights along sides of body
- lighted lure helps attract prey

11. Hatchet fish
- feeds on zooplankton and shrimp
- 3 to 4 inches long
- sides of body are silvery, with lights along belly

12. Mid-water jellyfish
- about 3 inches wide
- eats small fish and zooplankton
- body is maroon and white

13. Rattail fish
- about 2½ feet long
- body is gray
- feeds on lantern fish, shrimp, and the remains of dead animals

MIDNIGHT ZONE

14. Opossum shrimp
- 4 to 6 inches long
- body is red
- not a true shrimp

15. Snipe eel
- long jaws catch shrimp and zooplankton
- about 1½ to 3½ feet long
- body is brown or black

16. Black swallower
- about 6 inches long
- body is black
- can swallow fish that are 8 to 10 inches long
- stomach stretches to hold large prey

17. Vampire squid
- 5 to 8 inches long
- body is black with shades of purple
- body speckled with small lights
- not a true squid, but a close relative

18. Angler fish
- about 3 to 6 inches long
- body is dark brown or black
- eats fish, squid, zooplankton, and worms
- females have a light at the end of a stalk that helps them attract prey and mates

19. Tripod fish
- about 12 inches long
- body is dark brown
- long, stiff fins help it stand on soft bottom

20. Sea cucumber
- about a foot long
- crawls over bottom, feeding on small bits of food
- body is usually dark violet

B.

D.

F.

H.

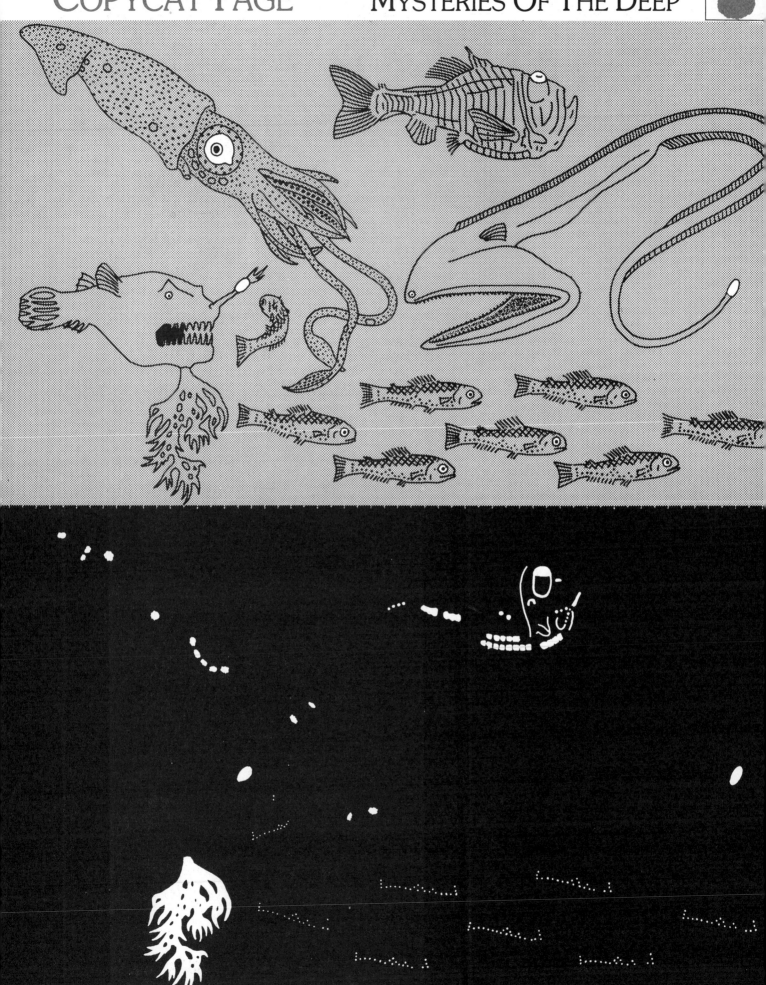

5 ft
68° F

100 ft
60° F

300 ft
56° F

1000 ft
44° F

3000 ft
43° F

6000 ft
38° F

9000 ft
37° F

15,000 ft
32° F

ALONG THE COAST & CLOSE TO SHORE

From the steep, rocky cliffs of northern California to the sandy shores of the Carolinas, land and sea meet to form many different kinds of coasts. In this chapter we'll take a closer look at these habitats. We'll also examine coral reefs and kelp forests—two shallow-water communities that border many of the world's coastal areas.

THE EDGE OF THE SEA

Many factors shape the "look" of a coast, including the material that makes up the land and the waves that hit the shore. And the nature of a coastal area influences the kinds of plants and animals that can live there.

COASTAL CONDITIONS

Tides and waves are two of the most important factors that shape the coast. Here's a closer look at each of these factors and how they affect life in coastal areas:

Washed by the Waves: Waves may crash violently against the coast or they may lap gently on the shore. They can carry debris and other material ashore, and they can carry sediment out to sea. Each year they strip sand away from certain areas and pile it up elsewhere. And over time they can wear rocky cliffs down to rubble.

Between the Tides: Along many coasts around the world, the tide rolls in and then out again twice each day. And twice each day the *intertidal zone*—the area between the high- and low-tide lines—is alternately covered with water and exposed to the air. As the water comes and goes, conditions such as temperature, moisture levels, and sometimes even salinity change.

Living on the Edge: Many animals, such as some fish and shorebirds, move into and out of intertidal areas as the tides rise and fall. But other living things are full-time residents and must cope with the waves, rising and falling tides, and other changing conditions that characterize these habitats. And depending on their ability to withstand these conditions, intertidal plants and animals may live farther away from or closer to the low-tide line. For example, organisms that live close to the low-tide line tend to be less able to deal with temperature extremes, desiccation, and other factors than organisms that live close to the high-tide line. Along many shores, particularly rocky shores, you can see distinct bands or zones of different species between the low- and high-tide lines.

COASTAL COMMUNITIES

Rocky Shores

Rocky shores, the sections of coast where rocky outcrops and ocean meet, stretch along many coasts around the world. But there are many different kinds of rocky shores. For example, much of the rocky coast of Maine slopes gently into the sea. But steep, rocky cliffs form much of the coast of the Pacific Northwest.

Marine plants and animals that live along rocky shores are adapted to a habitat that changes dramatically every day. For example, water levels along rocky shores may drop 12 feet or more between high and low tide. Marine organisms living on the rocks may be exposed to the air for 10 hours or more between high tides. And waves may strike the shore with incredible force.

Life on the Rocks: Rocky shores may be home to many different kinds of animals and plants. There may be seaweeds, such as rockweeds, sea palms, and Irish moss, as well as many other kinds of algae. Barnacles, rock-boring clams, sea urchins, chitons, sea stars, crabs, limpets, and many other animals may also live on

the rocks. Some of these animals graze on algae. Others filter food from the water. And some move across the rocks preying on other animals.

Withstanding Waves: How do marine plants and animals living in the rocky intertidal zone keep from being smashed to bits or torn from the rocks? They hold on tightly (barnacles, mussels, seaweeds), hide in cracks (crabs, brittle stars), and/or bend with the waves (seaweeds). In addition, many creatures' shells help them withstand and deflect the waves.

Coping with Tides: As the tide goes out, seaweeds growing in the intertidal zone droop against the rocks. Some of these plants can become almost completely dried out between tides with no "ill effects." Others stay moist under the protective blanket of larger seaweeds growing over them.

When the tide is out, most animals that live along rocky shores usually become inactive. For instance, periwinkles may pull their entire bodies into their shells, which keeps them from drying out. Many creatures, such as crabs and dog whelks, may crawl under a rock or moist seaweed, which helps them stay moist and avoid temperature extremes.

Pools of Life: Here and there along rocky coasts are depressions and crevices that stay filled with water as the tide goes out. Different kinds of plants and animals inhabit these *tide pools*, including algae, anemones, hermit crabs, sea stars, and even tiny fish. Depending on where a tide pool is in relation to the low-tide line, its conditions—and therefore the plants and animals that can live in it—may vary greatly. For example, tide pools that are high above the low-tide line are exposed to the air for relatively long periods of time between tides. The temperature and salinity in these pools fluctuates each day, depending on the air temperature, evaporation rate of the water, whether or not it's raining, and other factors. Only organisms that are adapted to widely fluctuating conditions live in these pools. Tide pools that are closer to the low-tide line are exposed to the air for shorter periods of time each day, experience less-fluctuating conditions, and support more life.

Beaches

Life on a beach is very different from that on a rocky shore. That's because the materials that make up a beach are always on the move. Whether a beach is made up of cobble, crushed shells, minute grains of sand, or some other material, wind and water shape and reshape it every day.

Because of their shifting substrates, beaches, in general, don't make very hospitable habitats. But some marine animals have found ways to cope with beach conditions—especially those of sandy beaches. Here the moist, relatively compacted sand provides a more stable environment than the looser, rough-and-tumble substrate of cobble, pebble, or other types of rocky beaches.

Digging In: To escape the substrate-shifting effects of wind, waves, and changing tides, most animals that are full-time residents of sandy beaches live underground. Some of these animals spend almost their entire lives buried in the sand. Other animals burrow into the sand only when the tide is low or to keep from being tossed around by waves.

Life Between the Grains: Clams, sand dollars, crabs, and certain other creatures live on or in sandy beaches. Some of these animals filter food from the water, others feed on tiny algae, bacteria, and other material among the sand grains, some prey on other animals, and some scavenge on material that washes ashore.

(continued next page)

Saltwater Wetlands

Stretching along much of the world's coasts are some of the most productive areas on Earth—salt marshes and mangrove swamps. For more about these habitats, see pages 18–32 of *NatureScope—Wading Into Wetlands* (Vol. 2, No. 5).

SUNKEN WORLDS

Coral reefs and kelp forests are two of the seas' richest communities. They form in waters that are usually no more than 130 feet deep and they're usually covered by water all of the time.

Coral Reefs

Coral reefs are created mainly by tiny, colonial animals called *corals*. They are home to brilliantly colored fish, animals that look like flowers, and thousands of other strange and colorful animals and plants. Corals live in oceans all over the world, but coral reefs form only in certain areas (see "Reefs of the World" on page 41).

Rock Makers: Stony corals, such as brain and elkhorn corals, are the reef-building corals. (They are also called *hard corals*.) These animals are able to take calcium and carbonate from seawater and crystallize them into limestone. Individual stony corals use the limestone to build protective rock cups around themselves. As a coral colony grows, the individual animals stay joined and the colony forms a solid mass of rock. New colonies grow over dead ones and eventually the huge mass of stone and living coral forms a reef. Sometimes reefs can grow until they stretch for hundreds of miles.

Vital Partners: Stony corals couldn't form the huge colonies characteristic of coral reefs if it weren't for the microscopic algae that live in their cells. Stony corals use oxygen and food that the algae produce during photosynthesis. And, for reasons scientists still don't understand, stony corals that have these algae in their cells secrete limestone at a much faster rate than stony corals that lack them. But even with algae in their cells, most stony corals secrete limestone at a fairly slow rate, and it takes thousands of years for a reef to form.

Coral Communities: By building the rocky foundation of coral reefs, stony corals inadvertently create living places for many other organisms. For example, anemones, soft corals, sponges, limestone-secreting algae, and many other plants and animals live attached to the limestone rock created by stony corals. Tube worms, sponges, and others excavate tunnels within the rock. And many kinds of fish, shrimp, crabs, and other creatures find food and shelter on a reef.

Wave Breakers: Besides being home to countless creatures, coral reefs are also coast protectors. As waves reach a reef's shallow waters, they break and lose their energy. Without the protection of a reef, many coastal areas would be much more subject to erosion by the waves.

Kelp Forests

In cold coastal waters, tall, brown algae called *kelp* may grow in such thick stands that they form underwater forests. In some ways these kelp forests are cold-water counterparts of coral reefs. Just like coral reefs, for instance, kelp forests grow on rocky bottoms in relatively shallow water and help protect the coast from waves. They are created by the growth of a particular kind of organism—in this case, kelp. And, most significantly, the growth of kelp creates living spaces for hundreds of different kinds of creatures.

But there are some distinct differences between kelp forests and coral reefs too. For one thing, the main "architects" of kelp forests are plants, not animals. And unlike corals, kelp can grow very quickly.

Some of the most extensive and well-known kelp forests grow in the waters off the coast of northwestern North America. But kelp forests exist in other parts of the world as well. For example, there are kelp forests off the coasts of Japan, South America, Great Britain, and New Zealand. (For more about kelp forests, see "Forests of the Sea" on page 43.)

Life Between the Tides

Perform chants about life on a rocky shore and sandy beach.

Objectives:
Name several organisms that live on a rocky shore or sandy beach. Describe how these organisms are adapted to their habitats.

Ages:
Primary and Intermediate

Materials:
- *copies of pages 48 and 49*
- *pictures of a rocky shore, sandy beach, and coastal inhabitants (see activity for specific species)*
- *large construction paper*
- *crayons or markers*
- *scissors*
- *glue*
- *reference books (optional)*

Subject:
Science

Battering waves, rising and ebbing tides, and constantly changing conditions characterize most coasts. In this activity your group will learn about some of the tricks coastal creatures use to cope with their special habitats.

First show the kids pictures of both rocky and sandy coasts. Use the background information on pages 36–37 to review the conditions that exist in each of these coastal habitats. During your discussion, ask the kids if they can think of ways the organisms in these habitats might keep from being washed away by waves. (On a rocky shore, many attach themselves firmly to rocks. And on a sandy beach, many burrow into the sand.) Then use the information under "Who's Who at the Coast" on page 40 to discuss each of the inhabitants of the rocky shore and sandy beach communities. Show the kids pictures of the animals and plants as you discuss them.

If you're working with older kids, you might want to have them research the shore organisms. They can work in research teams, and each team can be responsible for finding out how one of the plants or animals is adapted to its habitat. When the teams have finished researching, have them give presentations to the rest of the kids. They can make posters or models, write poems or stories that include natural history information about their organisms, or simply lead a discussion. Remind the kids that, whatever they choose to do, they should use pictures or diagrams during their presentations.

Now tell the kids to get ready for a "shore performance." Have each child take the part of one of the coastal creatures in the chants on page 40. (You can have several representatives for each animal or plant, depending on the number of kids in your group.) Help the kids learn their lines in the chants. Then have the "rocky shore" and "sandy beach" groups take turns performing their chants.

After the performance, pass out a copy of page 48 and 49 and two large sheets of construction paper to each child. Explain that the organisms shown in boxes on each page don't necessarily go with the scene they're drawn on. Have the kids color these pictures and cut them out. Also have them color the two scenes. Then tell the kids to glue each of the scenes onto a separate piece of construction paper. Have them match the animal and plant pictures to the appropriate scenes by gluing them around the construction paper "frame."

(continued next page)

Art Weber

ROCKY SHORE CHANT

REFRAIN (ALL SAY):
Let the waves crash all day—
Stuck on tight, we're OK.
We're STICK-TIGHTS!

BARNACLE KIDS:
We catch food with our feet.
Don't you think that's so neat?
We're BARNACLES!

REPEAT REFRAIN (ALL)

LIMPET KIDS:
We're protected so well
By a very hard shell.
We're LIMPETS!

REPEAT REFRAIN (ALL)

MUSSEL KIDS:
Our strong threads help us stay
So we don't wash away.
We're MUSSELS!

REPEAT REFRAIN (ALL)

ROCKWEED KIDS:
We're not animals; we're plants.
In the waves, watch us "dance."
We're ROCKWEED!

NWF file

SANDY BEACH CHANT

REFRAIN (ALL SAY):
Let the waves crash all day—
In the sand, we're OK.
We're DIGGERS!

SAND DOLLAR KIDS:
Since we're not really money,
Our name's kind of funny.
We're SAND DOLLARS!

REPEAT REFRAIN (ALL)

CLAM KIDS:
In the sand, we stay put
With a strong, digging foot.
We're CLAMS!

REPEAT REFRAIN (ALL)

MOLE CRAB KIDS:
We are named after moles
'Cause we dig lots of holes.
We're MOLE CRABS!

REPEAT REFRAIN (ALL)

LUGWORM KIDS:
We're like earthworms on land;
We dig tunnels in sand.
We're LUGWORMS!

WHO'S WHO AT THE COAST

ROCKY SHORE

BARNACLE
- a soft-bodied animal with a hard shell
- related to crabs, lobsters, and shrimp
- attaches itself with cement
- feeds during high tide by kicking out feathery legs and trapping plankton and other food
- closes up during low tide, which keeps it from drying out

LIMPET
- a soft-bodied animal with a cone-shaped shell
- a kind of sea snail
- its foot holds on tight with strong suction
- feeds during high tide by scraping up algae as it moves across rocks
- clamps down tight to a "home spot" during low tide, which keeps it from drying out or being swept away by waves

MUSSEL
- a soft-bodied animal with two shells that can close up
- related to clams
- attaches itself with strong threads it produces
- feeds during high tide by filtering plankton and tiny bits of food from the water

ROCKWEED
- a tough, smooth, slippery seaweed
- a kind of algae
- attached by a holdfast at its base
- droops against rocks during low tide
- buoyed up toward surface at high tide by air-filled bladders

SANDY BEACH

SAND DOLLAR
- a spiny-skinned animal
- a type of sea urchin
- traps bits of food with tube feet and short bristles
- "shovels" itself into sand

CLAM
- a soft-bodied animal with two shells that can close up
- uses a muscular foot to burrow into sand
- filters bits of food from the water

MOLE CRAB
- a soft-bodied animal with a hard shell
- related to crabs, but not a true crab
- burrows backwards into the sand
- extends eyes and feathery antennae above the sand
- uses antennae to trap tiny bits of food as waves wash over them

LUGWORM
- a segmented sea worm
- related to earthworms
- has short bristles along its body
- lives in a U-shaped burrow
- eats sand, from which it digests tiny bits of food

Note: Examples of all these creatures can be found on both the Atlantic and Pacific Coasts.

40

Reef Buddies

Make a wheel that shows some amazing coral reef partnerships.

Objectives:
Name several animals that depend on each other in a coral reef. Describe how these animals help each other.

Ages:
Primary and Intermediate

Materials:
- *copies of page 50*
- *copies of the "want ads" on page 42*
- *paper plates*
- *pictures of coral reefs*
- *crayons or markers*
- *scissors*
- *glue*
- *paper fasteners*
- *tape*
- *pushpin (optional)*

Subject:
Science

REEFS OF THE WORLD

Reef-building corals grow only where the water is warm (above 68° F), clear, and shallow enough for light to penetrate to the bottom. These conditions exist in tropical seas, generally around small islands and along the eastern shores of continents.

The largest and perhaps most well-known reef is the Great Barrier Reef, which stretches for over 1000 miles along the northeastern coastline of Australia. Other areas noted for their spectacular reefs are the Caribbean, the South Pacific, the Red Sea, and the Indian Ocean.

For many creatures in a coral reef, "you scratch my back and I'll scratch yours" is a way of life. By making "reef buddy" wheels, your group can learn about some amazing coral reef partnerships.

Before you begin, make several patterns for the kids to use in making their wheels. To do this, cut out the circle on page 50 and tape it to the middle of a paper plate. Stack this plate on top of two or more plates and cut out the four segments, leaving the center circle intact (see diagram below). Then remove the pictures from the pieces of the top paper plate and lay the patterns aside.

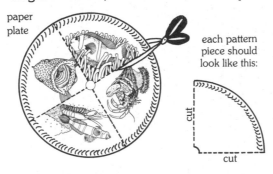

paper plate

each pattern piece should look like this:

cut

cut

Next show the kids pictures of coral reefs. Use the background information on page 38 and in the margin to review what these special habitats are and where they're found. Explain that some living things in a coral reef depend on other living things in a very close relationship. This special relationship is a type of *symbiosis*. (Symbiosis means "living together.")

Now pass out a copy of page 50, two paper plates, and a paper fastener to each child. Pass around the pattern pieces you made earlier and have the kids follow the steps below to make their reef buddy wheels.

After they've finished, use the information in "Partners For Life" on page 42 to go over each pair of reef buddies. (*Note:* You may want to have older kids make the pop-up coral reef craft on page 64 as a follow-up activity.)

HOW TO MAKE A REEF BUDDY WHEEL

1. Color the pictures on the Copycat Page and cut out the big circle along the dashed line.
2. Glue the circle to the middle of a paper plate, on the inside (the side you eat off of).
3. Lay this plate on top of the other plate. Poke a pushpin or scissors point through the center to make a small hole in both plates. Put the paper plate with the "reef buddy" pictures on it aside.
4. Lay the pattern on the plain paper plate, making sure the pattern edge is even with the edge of the plate. Trace around the pattern and cut out the wedge.
5. Draw a coral reef design on this plate with the wedge cut out.
6. Put the cut-out plate on top of the "reef buddy" plate. Finish the wheel by inserting the paper fastener through the center hole and secure in the back.

(continued next page)

finished wheel

Here's a fun way to reinforce what the kids have learned about coral reef partnerships. Make copies of the "want ads" below and pass them out to the kids. Have the kids try to identify which of the reef buddies might have placed each ad and which might have responded to each ad.

To do this they should match up the "box numbers" for each ad. For example, the first ad (box 1) represents an ad that an anemone might place. It goes with the ad in box 4, which represents a clownfish's ad. The kids could write "box 1/box 4" for their answer. (See answers in margin.)

THE REEF WEEKLY — WANT ADS

Safe and secure place for rent. I'll take in anyone that can keep unwanted company away. Write only if you can stand my "stinging" personality. Write: Coral Reef/Box 1

Seeking extra protection and a disguise. Willing to take on hitchhikers. Write: Coral Reef/Box 2

Need a cleaning? Count on me! I'll keep you spotless and healthy in exchange for meals. Write: Coral Reef/Box 3

Fish needs bodyguard and good home. (Not easily "stung.") Willing to help protect home from danger. Write: Coral Reef/Box 4

Strong digger in need of a "watchdog." Bonus: Plenty of extra space in my burrow. Write: Coral Reef/Box 5

Worried about safety? I can provide the added protection you need in exchange for a free ride around the reef. Write: Coral Reef/Box 6

In search of a personal groomer. I have a "tough guy" image, but with the right partner, I'm gentle as a lamb. Write if you want to eat in peace. Write: Coral Reef/Box 7

"Lookout" fish in search of a ready-made underground hideout. Lots of guard-duty experience. Write: Coral Reef/Box 8

Partners For Life

Clownfish and Sea Anemone: Several species of fish and invertebrates spend part or all of their lives in association with sea anemones. A clownfish, in fact, will never stray far from its anemone host. The fish avoids its enemies by staying nestled among the anemone's stinging tentacles. Scientists believe clownfish have a special mucous coating that prevents anemone stinging capsules from firing.

Many scientists think that the most important thing clownfish do for their anemone hosts is to protect them by chasing away animals such as butterfly fish, which often eat anemones.

Pistol Shrimp and Goby: In sandy areas of a coral reef, the pistol shrimp sometimes shares its burrow with a fish called a goby. The pistol shrimp spends most of its time digging and cleaning out its burrow. This shrimp finds food near the entrance of its home but can't sense when predators are near as well as the goby can. The goby hovers near the shrimp's burrow, and when a predator approaches, it flicks its tail and dives for cover inside the burrow. This signals danger and sends the shrimp down into the burrow too. Without the goby's alarm signal, the shrimp might not be able to escape danger in time.

Hermit Crab and Sea Anemone: A few species of hermit crabs—crabs that live in the empty shells of sea snails—usually have sea anemones attached to their shells. The anemones protect the crab from enemies—especially the octopus, which eats hermit crabs but is very sensitive to anemone stings. The anemones may also help camouflage the hermit crab.

Scientists aren't sure whether hermit crabs feed their anemone partners. But the anemones do get a free ride around the reef from the hermit crabs. By riding from place to place on top of a crab, an anemone probably gets scraps of food it might not have been able to get on its own.

Cleaner Fish and Grouper: Several species of small fish and shrimp perform a cleaning service for other fish. A cleaner fish usually stays in a small territory known as a cleaning station. When a potential "customer" enters the cleaning station, the tiny fish does a little "dance" identifying itself as a cleaner. The customer may be a large predator such as a grouper. But it recognizes the colors and movements of the cleaner fish and allows itself to be cleaned without harming the smaller fish. The cleaner fish even cleans up the wounds of reef fish, which helps them heal. In turn, the cleaner fish gets its food as it picks off pests and food particles from the larger animal's scales, mouth, and gills.

Forests of the Sea

Discuss kelp forests, then build a kelp forest model.

Objectives:
Compare a kelp forest with a forest habitat on land. Name several organisms that live in a kelp forest.

Ages:
Intermediate and Advanced

Materials:
- *copies of page 51*
- *copies of "Kelp Characters" on page 45*
- *easel paper*
- *large construction paper*
- *brown paper streamers*
- *pipe cleaners*
- *scissors*
- *glue*
- *tape*
- *crayons or markers*
- *pictures of kelp and kelp forests (optional)*
- *large drawing paper, clay, string, paint, stapler, old newspapers, toothpicks (optional)*

Subjects:
Science and Art

A type of seaweed called giant kelp can grow so densely in cool, coastal waters that it forms great underwater forests. In this activity your group can find out about the incredibly diverse community that these kelp forests support by building their own model of a kelp forest.

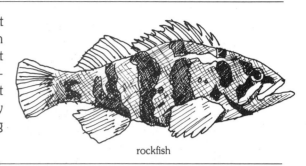
rockfish

CATCHING UP ON KELP

Before you get started, copy the kelp diagram in the margin on page 45 onto a sheet of easel paper. Also make copies of "Kelp Characters" on page 45. Then use the background information on page 38 to explain what kelp is and where it grows. If possible, show the kids pictures of kelp and kelp forests. Explain that, like trees in a forest on land, kelp grows in large stands. These stands are home to many different animals.

Next show the kids the diagram you copied earlier. Point out the blades, floats, stipe, frond, and holdfast and discuss how these parts might compare with parts of a tree (see "Close-Up on Kelp" on page 45).

Now pass out copies of page 51 and have the kids look at the kelp forest community. Also pass out the copies of "Kelp Characters" that you made earlier and have the kids read about some of the creatures that live in this community. Then ask them to locate each of these creatures on their Copycat Page.

Ask the kids if they can think of ways a kelp forest is similar to and different from a forest of trees. Use the information under "Close-Up on Kelp" to guide your discussion. Can the kids think of counterparts to kelp forest animals in a forest on land? (If you live near a woodlot, you might want to take the kids on a walk through the lot to look at forest layers and some of the animals that live in each one. For information about forest layers, see pages 34–35 of *NatureScope—Trees Are Terrific!* [Vol. 2, No. 1].)

After your discussion, have the kids color their kelp forest scene and kelp characters. Pass out a large sheet of construction paper to each child and have the kids glue their scene to the middle of their construction paper. Then tell them to cut apart the kelp characters and glue them onto the construction paper around the scene.

(continued next page)

Monterey Bay Aquarium
sea otter

BUILDING THE KELP FOREST

Now that the kids are familiar with some of the kelp forest inhabitants, they can turn part of the room into their own undersea forest. Here's how:

MAKING KELP

1. To make the stipes, cut lengths of streamers that match the distance from ceiling to floor.
2. To make blades, cut out long, narrow triangles from brown construction paper. Also cut a "float" at the wide end of each blade (see diagram). Tape the individual blades along the paper streamer stipes.
3. To make a holdfast, lay one end of a paper streamer stipe across the middle of a bundle of about five yellow pipe cleaners. Twist the bundle around the stipe. Then spread out the ends of the pipe cleaners, bending them to look gnarled and tangled.
4. Tape the finished kelp to the ceiling about two feet apart along one end of the room or in a corner. Gently twist the paper streamer stipes and let the pipe cleaner holdfasts rest on the floor.
5. Use various art supplies to create kelp forest creatures and place them in the proper layers of the paper kelp forest (see suggestions below).

MAKING KELP CREATURES

- To make a sea urchin, form a ball of clay about an inch in diameter and flatten it on one side. Break 15–20 toothpicks in half and poke the broken ends into the clay until the sea urchin is covered with "spines."
- To make a brittle star, form a small ball out of clay (about a half-inch to an inch in diameter) and flatten it to form the body. Stick five pipe cleaners (or shorter pieces of pipe cleaner of equal size) around the edge of the clay body and bend them to form the brittle star's arms.
- Cut small animals out of construction paper and tape them to the kelp stipes or hang them by pieces of string from the ceiling so they look like they're swimming among the fronds.
- To make a shark, sea otter, or other kelp forest predator, fold a large piece of paper in half. Draw the predator on the paper and cut out the shape so that you have two pieces. Glue or staple the two shapes together around the edges only, leaving an opening large enough to stuff. Color or paint both sides of the animal, then make your predator more three-dimensional by shredding some newspapers, crumpling the strips, and stuffing the strips into the opening. To finish up, glue or staple the open edge and hang the predator from the ceiling.
- For ideas on how to make crabs and snails from egg cartons, see page 26 of *NatureScope—Wading Into Wetlands* (Vol. 2, No. 5).

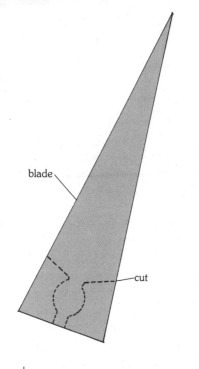

blade

cut

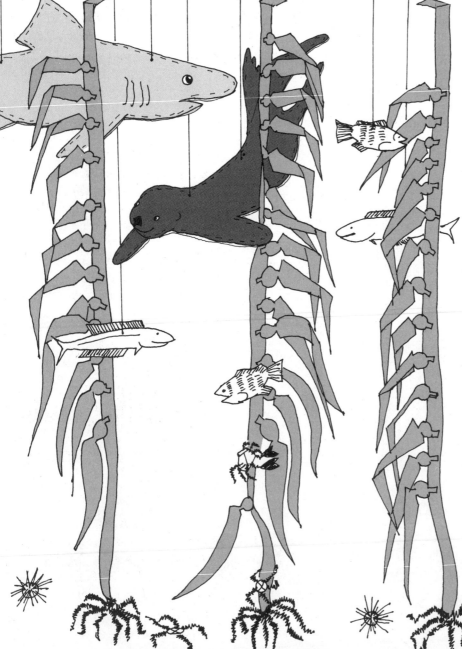

holdfast

CLOSE-UP ON KELP

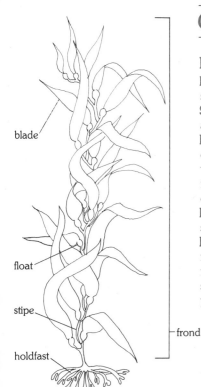

blade

float

stipe

holdfast

frond

KELP PARTS

Blade—leaflike structure that uses the sun's energy for photosynthesis

Stipe—stemlike structure that the blades are attached to

Float—air-filled bladder at the base of each blade that buoys the plant up toward the surface (By "reaching" for sunlit waters near the surface, kelp can gather light energy for photosynthesis.)

Frond—the collective name given to the stipe and blades of a single kelp plant

Holdfast—rootlike structure that sticks to rocks and other hard surfaces on the ocean floor (Unlike a root, the holdfast doesn't supply water and nutrients to the rest of the plant.)

KELP COMMUNITY

Like a forest on land, a kelp forest can be divided into layers. And you can find different kinds of animals in these different layers. At the bottom of the kelp forest, for example, brittle stars, sea urchins, and many other creatures live among the holdfasts. In the middle of the forest, snails and other animals crawl around on the blades and stipes. And many kinds of fish swim among the fronds.

The top layer of a kelp forest, like that of a forest on land, is called the *canopy*. Marine mammals, young fish, and seabirds spend time in this area. Some of these animals, as with some of the animals in the bottom and middle layers, also use other parts of the forest. Birds called cormorants, for example, dive down to hunt for fish among the fronds. And sea otters swim to the kelp forest floor to search for abalones and other food.

Note: The Monterey Bay Aquarium and *Project WILD Aquatic Education Activity Guide* have more kelp information and activities. To find out how to order these materials, see page 68.

KELP CHARACTERS

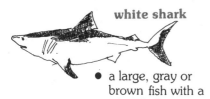

white shark

- a large, gray or brown fish with a white belly
- feeds mainly on fish and marine mammals
- sometimes hunts around the edges of kelp forests
- has no natural enemies

kelp crab

- color matches the kelp
- may attach bits of algae to its shell
- lives on stipes and feeds on kelp and tiny invertebrates
- eaten by sea otters, octopuses, and sea stars

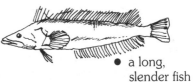

giant kelpfish

- a long, slender fish
- color changes to match its environment
- lives among the fronds, blending in with the swaying blades
- eats small fish, shellfish, crabs, and shrimp

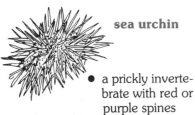

sea urchin

- a prickly invertebrate with red or purple spines
- lives at the base of kelp and feeds on all parts of the plant
- eaten by sea otters

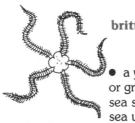

brittle star

- a yellow, brown, or green relative of sea stars and sea urchins
- has long, spiny arms
- lives in the holdfast region
- filters tiny bits of food from the water

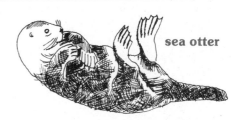

sea otter

- a mammal with thick, brown fur and webbed hind feet
- eats sea urchins, abalones, kelp crabs, and other invertebrates
- floats on its back at the surface, cracking open shellfish with rocks
- sometimes wraps itself and young in kelp (helps the animals stay put in the waves)

Seaside Adventure

Take a trip to the coast to explore a sandy beach or rocky shore.

Objectives:
Describe a coastal habitat. Name several coastal inhabitants and describe some of their adaptations.

Ages:
Primary, Intermediate, and Advanced

Materials (all optional):
- *field guides (see page 67 for suggestions)*
- *clipboards*
- *paper and pencils*
- *hand lenses*
- *enamel pan*
- *clear containers*
- *plastic bucket*
- *sieves or kitchen strainers*
- *shovels*
- *food coloring*
- *medicine dropper*
- *insect repellent*
- *sunscreen*
- *first-aid kit*
- *empty milk cartons*
- *heavy-duty plastic*
- *strong rubber bands*

Subject:
Science

There are over 88,000 miles of coastline in the United States, from sandy beaches to rocky palisades. If you can, take a trip to the shore with your kids so they can explore the special habitat where land meets sea.

Below are some guidelines you can use with the kids to help them get the most out of their trip. If you're working with older kids, you might want to use the guidelines to make up worksheets. You can also divide the group into investigation teams of three or four kids. And you might want to consider visiting the area several times during the year so the kids can compare their observations from different seasons.

COASTAL INVESTIGATIONS

AT A SANDY BEACH

Shore Material
- Using a hand lens, look closely at some sand grains. Describe their size, shape, and color.
- Compare sand from the upper and lower beach.

Tracks and Traces
- Examine marks on the sand. Watch creatures move and then investigate the tracks they leave.
- Draw any animal tracks that you find and, if you can, name the animals that made them.
- List or draw what you find in the debris that has washed up on the shore.

Sand Dwellers
- Scoop a shovelful of damp sand onto a sieve or kitchen strainer and see if any creatures are left behind after the sand sifts through.
- Add a shovelful of wet sand to a bucket of seawater and watch what swims out.
- Draw or describe each creature you find. Can you think of some ways each one is adapted to living in sand?

Study a Mole Crab
- Mole crabs are small, oval creatures. If you find one, put it *very gently* into a clear container filled with seawater. Describe how the mole crab behaves.
- Draw a picture of the mole crab and describe how its body is adapted to digging in sand.
- Next put the crab in a pan of seawater with an inch of sand in the bottom. Describe what happens.

AT A ROCKY SHORE

Shore Material
- Examine the rocks on the shore and describe their size, color, and texture.

Stick-Tights
- Draw several animals that are attached to the rocks.
- Describe differences you see between the attached animals that are underwater and any examples of the same species that are exposed to air.

Saltwater Plants
- Draw a picture of one kind of seaweed that's attached to the rock.
- Carefully lift up some seaweed that's draped across a rock above the water line and draw any living things you find on or under it.

Explore a Tide Pool
- Find a water-filled depression or crevice in a rock and observe what's in it. (You may want to make an underwater viewer by cutting the bottom out of a milk carton and securing heavy-duty plastic over one end with a strong rubber band.)
- Look for animals in your tide pool that crawl along or are attached to the bottom and draw a picture of one. If you can find them, also draw animals that swim and float.
- If there are any mussels in your tide pool, try this experiment. In a container, mix a little food coloring with some salt water. Use a medicine dropper to place one drop of the colored water next to the opened shell of a live mussel. What happened to the colored water? Why?

gannets

Leonard Lee Rue III

AT EITHER HABITAT

- Record the following: type of coast, location, date, time, tide (low, high, or in-between), wave conditions, and weather conditions.
- List or draw the different kinds of birds you see and describe where they are and what they're doing.
- Mark off a section of the shore from the water line to the high-tide line. Then look for distinct zones in this section marked by natural "boundaries" and describe these boundaries. (See "Things to Notice" under "Trip Tips," below.) List or draw the living things you find in each zone.
- Take a close-up look at plankton. (See page 27 for how to make a plankton net.)
- List any signs of human activity (besides those of your group) and describe the effect each activity has had on the environment.

TRIP TIPS

Getting Prepared: Before taking kids to the shore, become familiar with the area you plan to visit. (Avoid areas with sandbars, cliffs, caves, and other "kid-tempters.") Also be sure to get permission. And you may want to find out if there's a nearby nature center that can provide information or an on-site program for your group.

When scheduling your trip, be sure to check tide tables. Low tide is the best time to see marine creatures, and it's usually the safest time to be at the shore. Review with the kids what they can expect to see and do during their visit. ("Life Between the Tides" on page 39 makes a good introductory activity.)

What to Bring: Be sure to bring along plenty of containers so the kids can get a close-up look at the creatures they find. You may also want to bring hand lenses, shovels, and other equipment, depending on the investigations you plan to carry out.

If you're working with older kids, you should bring plenty of worksheets, pencils, and clipboards. (The kids can make their own clipboards by using rubber bands to secure their worksheets to pieces of cardboard.)

Things to Notice: As soon as you get to the shore, have the group observe the habitat quietly. Explain that they may see more animal activity if they observe the area *before* disturbing it.

Look for distinct bands or zones between the area exposed by low tide and the area above the high-tide line. On a rocky shore these zones are especially clear. Dark, crusty algae and lichens grow above the high-tide line, and barnacles and mussels grow farther down on the rocks. Various types of seaweed grow closest to the water.

On a sandy beach the zones aren't as distinctly divided. But locating the high-tide mark is usually easy on a sandy beach. Just look for the line of debris that was left behind by the waves of the highest tide. Beyond this high-water mark,

you'll often find sea grasses and other plants growing in the dry sand.

Back Where They Belong: After the kids have finished their investigations, have them replace their creatures where they found them. Also tell them to fill in any holes they've dug and to return any rocks they've overturned to their original positions.

Have a Safe Trip: By following these simple guidelines, your trip can be a safe and productive one:

- Provide plenty of adult supervision and have the kids work with partners.
- Explain that waves can be very dangerous. Have the kids try to face the water and be aware of the waves at all times.
- Tell the kids to watch their step when walking on rocks. Remind them that even rocks that look dry can be slippery.
- Take along a first-aid kit and some drinking water. And depending on the season, you may want to provide sunscreen or insect repellent.

COPYCAT PAGE

BETWEEN THE TIDES—SHEET 1

barnacle	sand dollar	lugworm	mussel

(See *Life Between the Tides*—p 39)

COPYCAT PAGE

limpet

rockweed

clam

mole crab

(See *Life Between the Tides*—p 39)

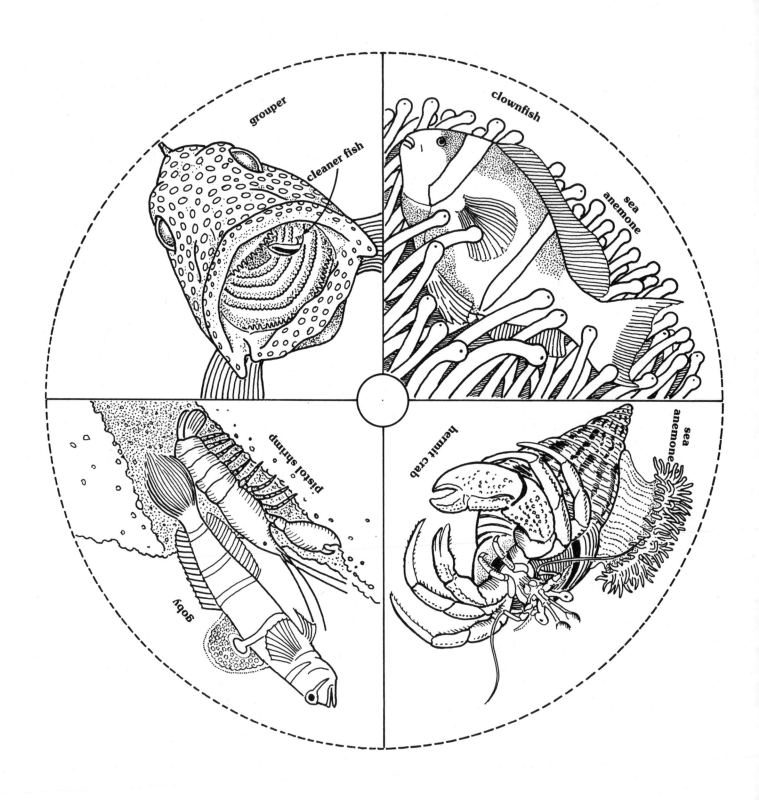

grouper

clownfish

cleaner fish

sea anemone

pistol shrimp

goby

hermit crab

sea anemone

RANGER RICK'S NATURESCOPE: DIVING INTO OCEANS

(See *Reef Buddies*—p 41)

PEOPLE AND OCEANS

*I*t's so bad you don't know what's coming in with the next tide. That's how one person described the situation along the New Jersey coast during the summer of 1987. But the problem she was referring to—beach-bound garbage washing in with the surf—isn't restricted to the New Jersey shore. It's occurring on beaches all over the world.

The influx of garbage on beaches is just one of many ocean-related problems we're facing today. But our relationship with the ocean isn't all "bad news." People studying the ocean are making new discoveries all the time about how the Earth "works," how to use the ocean's resources, and how to solve some of the problems we've created. In this chapter we'll look at some of the most serious ocean problems, people's relationship with the sea through time, and some exciting ideas about the future of ocean technology.

POLLUTING THE SEA

As long as there have been human settlements along coasts, people have been dumping garbage and other refuse into the ocean. And although these pollutants often caused problems in the past for marine communities (and even some of the human communities responsible for them), they usually didn't do permanent damage to the ocean. Now, though, the amount of pollution pouring into the ocean is greater than it's ever been. And some of the modern pollutants are much more harmful than those of the past.

Garbage Goes Overboard: Trash, the most visible form of ocean pollution, comes from several different sources. Military, trade, fishing, and recreational ships, for example, regularly unload garbage into the water. And manufacturing plants often dump trash and other waste either directly into the ocean or into rivers or other ocean-bound tributaries.

One reason ocean garbage is coming back to haunt us on beaches in ever-increasing quantities has to do with the rising volume of trash we're producing. In 1960, each person in the United States generated an average of about three pounds of trash per day. In 1987, the figure per person was up to about five pounds per day (and the population had increased by more than 60 million people). We're running out of places on land to put all of our waste—so we've been turning more and more to the sea.

The Throw-away Lifestyle: The nature of trash itself these days is also a big contributor to the problem of ocean garbage. Next time you walk along a beach, take a look at the debris that has collected at the high-tide line. Chances are much of it will be made of plastic: soft-drink containers, old fishing line, six-pack holding rings, and an odd assortment of other plastic items—from toothbrushes to toys. Most plastic doesn't break down for hundreds of years or longer, so the plastic we're dumping at sea today could hang around for generations.

For ocean wildlife, plastic is bad news. Annually, about two million seabirds, 100,000 marine mammals, and countless other sea animals die after accidentally eating plastic or getting tangled in it. (For more about the effects of plastic pollution on wildlife, see "Plastic in the Sea" on page 59.)

Slicks at Sea: Oil pollution is another problem in oceans around the world. It comes from several different sources. Accidents involving offshore rigs and tankers, for example, can cause devastating oil spills. Ships also discharge a lot of oil

Nova Scotia Information Service

into the sea. But oil-laden waters that wash into the sea from city streets and other places may account for much of the oil pollution in coastal areas. (For more about pollutants that wash into the sea from land, see "It All Ends Up in the Water" below.)

Oil can poison marine organisms outright, and when oil coats feathers or fur it can interfere with an animal's natural insulation. When this happens, the animal can die of exposure.

Ocean Cesspools: In many areas these days, a visit to the shore can be hazardous to your health. The reason is sewage. The surf that laps some of the balmy shores of the Mediterranean Coast, for example, is laced with the stuff. And certain harbors in Boston, New York, and many other cities around the world have become cesspools.

Much of the sewage reaching coastal waters is untreated—that is, it flows directly from sewers into the ocean without first being made less noxious at a sewage treatment plant. And the situation often gets worse during storms: Floods can make sewers and treatment plants back up and overflow, causing more untreated sewage to wash straight into the sea.

Sewage contains bacteria that can severely contaminate an area and the organisms that live there—including shellfish and other seafood animals. Cases of hepatitis, cholera, and other diseases seem to be on the rise in some regions, and many scientists feel that sewage contamination is the culprit.

It All Ends Up in the Water: As bad as sewage, trash, and certain other kinds of pollution can be, there's one type of ocean pollution that may prove to be far more damaging to some coastal areas—particularly bays and estuaries. This is the pollution caused by *runoff*, the collective name given to the polluted water that washes into bodies of water from farms, highways, city streets, suburban lawns, and construction sites.

Fertilizers, oil, pesticides, salt, silt, and all kinds of other residues and chemicals contribute to polluted runoff—and each is harmful in its own way. Fertilizers, for example, pollute by providing too much of a good thing: nutrients. When fertilizers laden with phosphorus, nitrogen, and other nutrients wash into a body of water, algae and certain other organisms take advantage of the glut. They grow and reproduce like crazy, often causing what's known as an *algal bloom*. And as they "bloom" and eventually die, oxygen supplies in the water become depleted, sometimes suffocating fish and other animals. (Oxygen depletion can also result from sewage, which acts as a kind of super fertilizer.)

RISING TO MEET THE CHALLENGE

No matter how we decide to deal with ocean problems, we've got our work cut out for us. Besides those we've already talked about, there are others: overfishing, coastal erosion, the dumping of radioactive wastes, mining at sea. Many of these problems and issues aren't well understood, and most don't seem to have any quick-and-easy fixes. But accepting the challenge to find solutions is the only choice we have that makes sense. The ocean is too important to people in too many ways for us to let our activities get the better of it.

Positive Steps: Fortunately, people *are* making some moves toward solving ocean problems. For example, if it weren't for regulations to control pollution near coasts and protect marine animals, many coastal areas and certain species of marine wildlife would be in far worse shape than they are now. And new laws are in the works, such as a recent treaty designed to restrict the dumping of plastic at sea. Also, recycling is starting to catch on in some areas—and the more we recycle, the less garbage we'll end up generating.

New Approaches: On another level, researchers are working on some innovative approaches that could help solve ocean problems. Biodegradable plastic is being tested, for one thing. Ideas for what to do with sewage to make it less noxious are also being studied. And in the future, scientists may be able to use oil-consuming bacteria to clean up oil spills.

WHERE WE'VE BEEN; WHERE WE'RE GOING

Would Christopher Columbus or Ferdinand Magellan have become world explorers if they hadn't had seas to set sail on? Would trade between nations have gotten anywhere without routes of travel across oceans? These are impossible questions to answer, of course, because it is impossible to separate people's lives—and for that matter, civilization in general—from the influences of the sea. The ocean has been an avenue for exploration and trade for millennia, not to mention an important source of food, a huge scientific laboratory, and a playground for vacationers. It's set the scene for works of literature, served as a home for mermaids and other creatures of sailors' imaginations, and made heroes out of adventurers, pilgrims, and anyone else willing to brave its vast, empty stretches and thrashing waves.

Waves of the Future: As we move into the twenty-first century, you can look to the sea to play an even bigger role in our lives. Picture, for example, ocean farms designed to rear fish or cultivate algae for an ever-increasing human population. And imagine having your home heated with energy harnessed from a surging surf.

You can also expect to see technology, medicine, and other fields benefiting from advances originating in the sea. For example, researchers are working on efficient ways of converting salt water into large amounts of fresh water. And before too long, physicians might be able to replace damaged bones with a bone substitute made from algae.

If we start taking better care of the ocean, there's no doubt that our relationship with it will become even more enriching and complex. There's a whole ocean of opportunities within the salty waters that cover almost three-quarters of the planet.

Mythical Monsters

Talk about sea myths, then write descriptions of mythical creatures based on real marine animals.

Objectives:
Name a mythical marine creature. Describe one possible origin of this creature.

Ages:
Primary and Intermediate

Materials:
- *pictures of marine plants and animals (see activity for suggestions)*
- *writing paper*
- *drawing paper*
- *pencils*
- *markers or crayons*
- *examples of sea myths (optional)*
- *reference books (optional)*

Subjects:
Science and Language Arts

Sailors in the 16th and 17th centuries told hair-raising tales of the dreaded kraken—one of the most terrifying monsters in the sea. With its hundred-foot-long arms, the kraken could capsize ships or pluck sailors from the tallest masts. Today, many people agree that the monstrous kraken is an exaggerated version of a real ocean animal, the giant squid.

You can challenge your kids' imaginations by having them make up their own sea myths. Before you begin the activity, find pictures of several different marine plants and animals. (The kids will be using them later.) You'll need one plant or animal for every four kids in your group. (You won't need as many if you're working with young kids.) Organisms with good "myth potential" include the narwhal, sawfish, white shark, Portuguese man-of-war, hammerhead shark, giant clam, manta ray, walrus, lobster, ocean sunfish, moray eel, whale shark, sargassum, and giant kelp.

To get the kids into a "mythical mood," begin by talking about mermaids, sea serpents, and other well-known mythical creatures. (You may want to read a myth such as "The Little Mermaid" by Hans Christian Anderson to young kids, and excerpts from *Twenty Thousand Leagues Under the Sea* by Jules Verne to older groups.) Tell the kids that some sea myths may be based on exaggerated descriptions of real animals. For example, mermaids may be based on seals, walruses, or manatees; sea serpents may have their origins in the giant squid or oarfish; leviathans may be based on huge whales; and so on. Also tell the kids that myths were probably first created by people who saw strange sights that they couldn't explain. For example, a weary sailor who saw a strange shape in stormy seas might think it was a sea monster. And as the story of the monster sighting was retold, some details (such as the creature's size and behavior) might have been exaggerated.

If you're working with older kids, divide them into teams of four. Then give each team one of the animal or plant pictures that you gathered earlier. Explain that, as a group, each team will get a chance to create a myth based on their plant or animal. In their myth, they can exaggerate some of the organism's features. (They might want to do some research on their organism to find out more about its natural history.) For example, the giant kelp could become a monstrous, people-eating seaweed that engulfs passing ships and their crews. The kids can also name their newly created creatures and illustrate their tales. Afterward they can take turns sharing their myths.

If you're working with younger kids, make up exaggerated descriptions about some of the real animals and plants you've gathered pictures of. For example, you could describe the manta ray as "a huge black beast that flies through the water flapping its wide, dark wings. Like a big bat, it swoops out of the water and glides past ships. A long, thin tail stretches out behind the creature and whips around to sting anything within its reach." Have the kids draw what they think the creature looks like, then show them pictures of the real animal or plant.

THE BETTMANN ARCHIVE, INC.

Globetrotters

Play a team game about ocean exploration.

Objectives:
Describe several historic events in ocean exploration. Plot points on a world map using latitude and longitude.

Ages:
Advanced

Materials:
- *copy of the facts and ships on page 58*
- *world map showing latitude and longitude*
- *straight pins or tape*
- *easel paper*
- *scissors*
- *small world maps (optional)*

Subjects:
Science, Geography, and History

Many people know that a spacecraft carried the first people to the moon in 1969. But not as many people are aware of the 1960 voyage to the deepest known spot in the ocean. By playing a team game, your group can learn about historic ocean events and about some of the people who made them happen. They'll also get to bone up on their map-reading skills.

Before playing the game, make a copy of the facts and ships on page 58. Cut the facts apart and put them into a sack. Color the two ships and cut them out. Then put a large world map that shows latitude and longitude where everyone can see it. Finally copy the points of each route shown on the next page onto a sheet of easel paper and put the sheet in a prominent place. (*Note:* You may also want to provide smaller copies of a world map so all the kids can work on their mapping skills at the same time during the game.)

Now begin the activity by telling the kids that people have been exploring the oceans for centuries. Some have made geographic discoveries and others have made important scientific discoveries.

Next tell the kids that they're going to play a game to discover the routes of two famous exploration voyages around the world. They'll also learn about other important ocean events and explorers as they plot points on a world map.

Divide your group into two teams. Explain that one team will follow the route of the first voyage around the world, led by Ferdinand Magellan in 1519. (Magellan was searching for a shorter route to Asia. He was wrong about the shortcut, but he became the first European to cross the Pacific Ocean. And he discovered an important passage to the Pacific at the tip of South America, now known as the Strait of Magellan.) The other team will track the first round-the-world research voyage, made by the crew of the HMS *Challenger* from 1872 to 1876. (Scientists on board the *Challenger* studied the physical and biological characteristics of the world's oceans. Their work marked the beginning of modern oceanography.)

Review latitude and longitude with the kids so they'll know how to plot points on the map. You can plot the starting point for each voyage to help them get the hang of it. For example, tell the kids that Magellan started his voyage from around 37°N, 6°W. Show them how to find that location on the map you put up earlier. Point out the country and have the kids identify it. (Spain) Then attach your copy of Magellan's ship to the map at that point with a straight pin or piece of tape. Next explain that the picture of the *Challenger* should be attached at 51°N, 1°W. Have the kids identify where that voyage began. (England)

Now refer to the points of the two travel routes that you put up earlier. Explain that the teams will be using these points to move their ships around the world. Then follow the steps on the next page and let the two teams "set sail."

ALVIN (a submersible)

HOW TO PLAY "GLOBETROTTERS"

ANSWERS

1000: Greenland
1492: Bahamas
1513: Panama
1773: Antarctic Circle
1786: Gulf of Mexico
1831: Andes
1840: Antarctica
1866: Newfoundland
1872: Italy
1892: France
1905: California
1925: Germany
1930: Massachusetts
1934: Bermuda
1943: Mediterranean
1960: Guam
1969: Morocco
1970: Caribbean
1974: Atlantic
1975: North Carolina
1977: Galapagos
1979: Hawaiian
1985: Atlantic
1985: Florida

1. Have two members from the Magellan team come up to the map. One person can draw a fact from the "fact sack" and the other person can read it out loud.

2. Have the two members try to answer the question asked in their fact by locating the point on the map indicated by the latitude and longitude clues (see answers in margin). To keep the game going at a good pace, time the teams. (You might want to give each pair of kids about 30 seconds per play.)

3. If their answer is correct, they may attach the fact to the map at the correct point and move their team's ship to the first point on Magellan's route. (They'll have to locate this point using latitude and longitude too.) If their answer is incorrect, their fact goes back in the sack and their ship stays where it is. After the first team's play, it's the *Challenger* team's turn.

4. Continue having the two teams take turns answering the questions, plotting the points, and moving their ships until one team wins by completing its round-the-world voyage. *Note:* For the approximate routes, see the map below.

Magellan's Route	Route of the *Challenger*
start: 37°N, 6°W	start: 51°N, 1°W
1: 5°N, 15°W	1: 5°S, 35°W
2: 8°S, 35°W	2: 35°S, 20°E
3: 52°S, 68°W	3: 65°S, 80°E
4: 40°S, 80°W	4: 40°S, 174°E
5: 24°S, 100°W	5: 20°N, 112°E
6: 2°N, 170°W	6: 3°S, 145°E
7: 10°N, 124°E	7: 35°N, 140°E
8: 3°S, 126°E	8: 20°N, 155°W
9: 30°S, 90°E	9: 35°S, 75°W
10: 35°S, 20°E	10: 52°S, 68°W
11: 40°N, 30°W	11: 35°S, 57°W
end: 37°N, 6°W	end: 51°N, 1°W

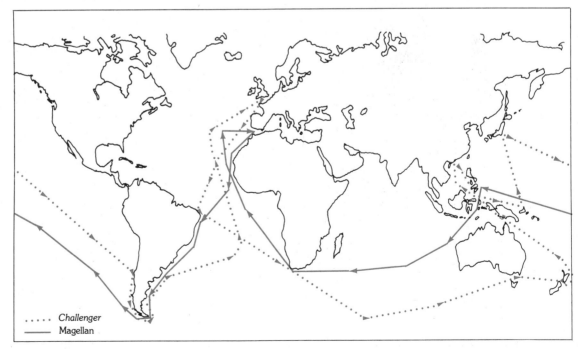

····· Challenger
——— Magellan

(continued next page)

EXPLORATION CLUES

1000: Many people believe the Vikings discovered America long before Columbus did. We know that Eric the Red got as far as what large island? (70°N, 40°W)

1492: Christopher Columbus reached the New World—now called the Americas—by sailing west across the Atlantic Ocean in search of a new route to Asia. The first island he landed on is in what island chain? (24°N, 74°W)

1513: The first European to see the Pacific Ocean was Vasco de Balboa. What country did he cross to see it? (8°N, 80°W)

1773: Captain James Cook sailed in search of a "southern continent." He never saw it, but while searching, he became the first person to cross what major latitude line? (66°S)

1786: Ben Franklin published the first map of the Gulf Stream to help sailors cross the ocean. The Gulf Stream originates in what body of water? (25°N, 90°W)

1831: Starting from England, naturalist Charles Darwin went on a world-wide research voyage aboard the HMS *Beagle*. He discovered fossil seashells 12,000 feet high in what mountain range? (33°S, 72°W)

1840: Charles Wilkes of the U.S. Navy proved the existence of a seventh continent by leading an expedition there. What is the seventh continent? (70°S, 135°E)

1866: The first successful transatlantic cable was laid across the ocean floor. Depth charts developed by Matthew Maury helped people know where to lay the cable. It stretched from Ireland to what Canadian province? (48°N, 56°W)

1872: Anton Dohrn founded the first marine biological station. This research laboratory is in what country? (42°N, 14°E)

1892: Louis Boutan took the first underwater photographs. What country was Boutan from? (45°N, 4°E)

Magellan

Challenger

1905: Scripps Institution of Oceanography was founded. Many ocean research scientists work here. What state is Scripps in? (35°N, 120°W)

1925: A research ship named the *Meteor* crisscrossed the South Atlantic Ocean to survey it with echo sounding. What country did the *Meteor* belong to? (50°N, 10°E)

1930: Woods Hole Oceanographic Institute was founded. Many ocean research scientists work here. What state is Woods Hole in? (43°N, 71°W)

1934: William Beebe descended a half-mile into the ocean depths in a steel ball called a *bathysphere*. This deep-sea dive took place near what island? (32°N, 65°W)

1943: Jacques Cousteau developed the *aqualung*. The aqualung enables divers to carry their own air supply underwater. In what sea was this new invention tested? (40°N, 5°E)

1960: Jacques Piccard descended to the deepest known spot in the ocean in a submarinelike ship called the *Trieste*. This spot is nearly seven miles below the surface in the Mariana Trench. It's located at the bottom of the ocean near what island? (14°N, 145°E)

1969: Thor Heyerdahl sailed across the Atlantic Ocean in a reed raft called *Ra II* to show that sailors from ancient Africa also could have done so. What African country did he sail from? (33°N, 7°W)

1970: Sylvia Earle led the first all-woman team of U.S. aquanauts. (Aquanauts are divers who live in an undersea laboratory and study the ocean while scientists on the surface study the divers' ability to live and work underwater.) Earle's team spent two weeks in the underwater station called *Tektite II* near a group of islands in what sea? (15°N, 65°W)

1974: Robert Ballard explored a volcanic mid-ocean ridge in a small submersible called *Alvin*. He saw lava oozing from an area where two plates of the Earth's crust are spreading apart. In which ocean was this discovery made? (38°N, 32°W)

1975: The United States established the first National Marine Sanctuary to protect the wreck of a Civil War ship that sank in an 1862 storm. The ship, called the *Monitor*, was discovered off the barrier islands of what state? (36°N, 76°W)

1977: Robert Ballard explored a mid-ocean ridge in a small submersible called *Alvin* and discovered an unusual community in the dark ocean depths. This community lives where heat from the Earth's core is released through vents. Giant tube worms and other strange creatures are part of this community. Near what group of islands was the community first discovered? (1°S, 91°W)

1979: Sylvia Earle dove to the ocean floor inside an armored suit called a Jim suit. The Jim suit is like a one-person submersible. Earle went to a depth of 1250 feet—the deepest any person has ever been without being connected to a boat with a line. Near what islands did she make this historic dive? (20°N, 155°W)

1985: An undersea robot called *Argo* located the wreck of the *Titanic* at the bottom of the ocean. (The *Titanic* was a luxury ocean liner that hit an iceberg and sank in 1912.) In what ocean was the wreck found? (42°N, 50°W)

1985: A treasure hunter located millions of dollars' worth of silver, gold, and gems from the wreck of a Spanish galleon. The ship sank in a 1622 storm off the coast of what state? (25°N, 82°W)

Plastic in the Sea

Discuss plastic pollution and interpret data about plastic dumping in the ocean.

Objectives:
List several ways ocean dumping harms wildlife. Describe several ways people can cut back on their use of plastic.

Ages:
Intermediate and Advanced

Materials:
- *copies of pages 62 and 63*
- *chalkboard or easel paper*
- *graph paper*
- *paper and pencils*

Subjects:
Science and Social Studies

Items Collected in 1986 Texas Coast Cleanup

Material	Number of Items	% of Total
plastics	95,560	56%
rubber	20	0.01%
glass	20,040	12%
Stryofoam	19,280	11%
metal	22,100	13%
paper	10,340	6%
wood	4160	2%

Data courtesy of the Center for Marine Conservation, Washington, DC.

 very year, approximately 14 billion pounds of tires, cardboard boxes, plastic cups, bottles, and other trash are dumped into the ocean. Some of the trash sinks, some of it is eaten by ocean creatures, and a lot of it—especially the plastic—floats. All of the trash can create problems for wildlife and people. But the floating plastic, most of which takes years to break down, can be especially harmful. Your group can find out why plastic dumping is a problem by interpreting data from a beach cleanup and by investigating their own use of plastic.

PART 1: PUTTING PLASTIC IN PERSPECTIVE

Start by telling the group they are going to explore some of the problems that occur because of ocean dumping—in particular, the dumping of plastic. To find out what your kids already know about ocean dumping, divide the group into teams of four or five and give each team the following questions to discuss:
- What types of trash have they seen washed up on the beach? What's the most common material? (If they haven't been to a beach, ask them to list things they think might wash up onto beaches.)
- How do they think the trash got on the beach?
- How do they think their community disposes of trash?
- What are some ways that ocean dumping harms people and wildlife?

After the teams have had a chance to discuss these questions, have each team present their answers to the rest of the kids. Then lead a discussion about wastes and waste-dumping, using the following information:
- Trash is disposed of in several different ways. Some trash is burned in incinerators and some is carted away to landfills. And garbage on ships is often simply dumped into the ocean.
- Plastics, metals, chemicals, paper, food, and many other types of wastes are dumped into the ocean.
- Ocean dumping can harm wildlife in many ways. For example, dumping toxic chemicals into water can poison fish, shellfish, and other creatures. And plastic waste can cut, tangle, poison, and strangle turtles, seabirds, sea mammals, and other marine life. (See page 63 for more about the ways plastic can harm wildlife.)
- More than half of the trash that washes up on beaches is plastic. (Many plastics float, and many don't break down for hundreds of years or longer.)

Now tell the kids they're going to take a statistical look at some trash that ended up on a Texas beach. Write the data in the margin on a chalkboard or piece of easel paper and explain that it is actual data from the 1986 cleanup of a Texas beach. For older kids, leave out the percentages and have the kids calculate them. Then have them graph their results in a bar or pie graph (see diagram).

Next pass out copies of page 62 and have the kids use the graphs to answer the questions on the side of the page. (See answers at the end of the activity.)

(continued next page)

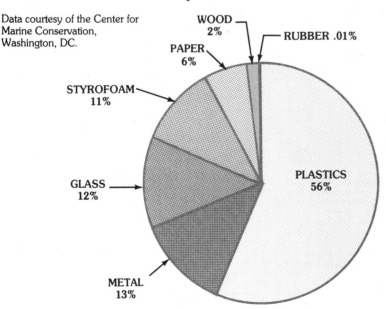

WOOD 2% — RUBBER .01% — PAPER 6% — STYROFOAM 11% — GLASS 12% — METAL 13% — PLASTICS 56%

PART 2: PLASTIC IN OUR LIVES

To help get your kids thinking about how prominent plastic is in our daily lives, try these activities:

Plastic Supermarkets: Take your group on a trip to a supermarket to have them "check out" food packaging. Divide the group into teams of four or five and assign each team a different aisle to investigate. Tell them to make a list of the types of grocery items they see and how each one is packaged. To show the kids that plastic wrapping is often "hidden," you might want to buy one or two items that are packaged in cardboard with plastic liners inside. (Examples include certain types of cereals and frozen pouch dinners.) If it's too difficult to get your group to a supermarket, you can make assignments and have the kids go to the store with their parents or just look at products they have at home.

Plastic Journals: Have each person keep a journal for several days. Ask the kids to keep track of the types of products they use every day, and what types of plastic products they throw away. Also have them note how other people use and dispose of plastic.

Things to Think About: After doing the two previous activities, have the group break up into their original teams. Then pass out copies of the plastic facts on page 63. Have the kids use the facts on the sheet, as well as the information they gathered in the supermarket search and by keeping journals, to help them brainstorm some ideas about the following:

- What are some ways that people can cut down on the amount of plastic they use? What are some alternatives to plastic products?
- What are some ways plastic is harmful to wildlife?
- Will sponsoring beach cleanups solve the problem of plastic pollution? Why or why not?
- If you could pass a law in your community about plastic trash disposal or cleanup, what would the law say?
- What type of plastic-related research would you like to see conducted?

BRANCHING OUT: CLEAN UP YOUR BEACH

Sponsoring a beach cleanup is a terrific way to introduce your community to the problems of ocean dumping. Many coastal states have regular beach cleanup programs and Adopt-A-Beach programs that you can get involved with. In addition, many communities sponsor cleanups of stream, river, and lake shorelines.

For more information about cleanups in your state or for information about how your group might initiate its own cleanup, contact one of these organizations:

California Coastal Commission
631 Howard St., 4th Floor
San Francisco, CA 94105

Center for Marine Conservation
1725 DeSales St., NW
Suite 500
Washington, DC 20036
(There's also an office at 1201 West 24th St., Austin, TX 78705.)

Chesapeake Bay Foundation
162 Prince George St.
Annapolis, MD 21401

Clean Ocean Action
P.O. Box 505
Highlands, NJ 07732

Oregon Department of Fish and Wildlife
P.O. Box 59
Portland, OR 97207

Save the Bay, Inc.
434 Smith St.
Providence, RI 02908-3732

For another plastic-related activity, see "Plastic Jellyfish" on page 159 in the *Project WILD Aquatic Education Activity Guide*. See page 68 for more information.

Answers:
1. 1975–1980
2. about seven times higher or about 49,000 million pounds
3. about 142% or approximately 33,000 million pounds
4. graph #1 (production of plastic); plastic is being used to make other products besides packaging
5. about 41,000 million pounds; boats, toys, cars, appliances, and so on
6. Will continue to show an increase. If people change their plastic-use habits, the rate might not increase as dramatically as it has in the past. If new types of synthetic materials are developed to replace plastic, plastic production might decrease accordingly.

Sea of Many Uses

Research some of the many ways people use the ocean.

Objectives:
Name some ways people use the ocean. Name some possible future uses of the ocean. Discuss some of the ways people's activities affect the ocean.

Ages:
Advanced

Materials:
- *copies of "Topics to Tackle"*
- *reference books*
- *art supplies (optional)*

Subjects:
Social Studies, History, and Science

 ere's a way to help your kids learn more about how people use the ocean and how our activities affect it. Divide the group into research teams of three or four kids and assign each team (or let each team choose) one of the research topics listed below. Tell the kids that they'll be preparing reports on their topics and that each team will be presenting the information to the rest of the kids.

Make copies of the discussion points and questions listed under each topic and hand them out to the appropriate teams. Explain that the kids should use the discussion points and questions as guidelines while they're doing their research, but that they can include any other information in their reports that they feel is important.

Point out that many of the topics the kids will be researching are currently in the news, and that traditional sources of information, such as encyclopedias, may not have the most up-to-date information about them. So encourage the kids to also use the *Reader's Guide to Periodical Literature.*

Depending on the number of kids you're working with, you might want to add extra research topics. Here are some possibilities: sea exploration (its history and future possibilities); the ocean's role in the arts (literature, music, painting, and other art forms); whaling; fishing rights; and products we get from the sea (medicines, pearls, sponges, and so on).

As the kids work on their presentations, encourage them to develop interesting "visuals." They could make large charts or graphs, show pictures, make models, or do demonstrations. For example, the desalinization team could design a simple apparatus to show how fresh water can be obtained from salt water through boiling or solar heating.

TOPICS TO TACKLE

Mariculture (Ocean Aquaculture)
- Discuss the history of mariculture.
- Discuss current uses and practices of mariculture.
- How might mariculture be used in the future?
- Are there any environmental drawbacks to large-scale maricultural practices? Discuss any you come up with.

Desalinization (Fresh Water from the Sea)
- Describe some of the ways fresh water can be obtained from the sea.
- How could people benefit from large-scale desalinization?
- Why isn't desalinization a bigger industry than it is?
- Discuss how desalinization might be made more effective.
- What are some possible environmental consequences to consider if desalinization becomes a more important industry? (Think about how large amounts of fresh water would be obtained, how it might be used, and how it could change natural communities.)

Ocean Fishing
- What are some of the foods we get from the sea?
- Discuss the nutritional value of some seafoods.
- Name several countries in which ocean fishing is a major industry.
- Describe several methods of catching ocean fish.
- Discuss some of the negative effects ocean fishing has had on fish populations and on other wildlife such as porpoises.

Mining at Sea
- Do we get any minerals from the ocean? If so, what are they and how are they obtained?
- Discuss the minerals we could get from the ocean floor in the future and how these minerals might be used.
- Discuss problems associated with ocean mining. (Think about issues such as environmental disturbances that could result from mining operations and who owns mineral rights in certain areas.)

Ocean Energy
- Discuss ocean tides as a source of energy and the advantages and disadvantages of harnessing this type of energy.
- Discuss ocean waves as a source of energy and the advantages and disadvantages of harnessing this type of energy.
- Discuss thermal energy in the ocean and the advantages and disadvantages of harnessing this type of energy.

Ocean Pollution
- Discuss some of the different kinds of ocean pollution (garbage, oil, sewage, runoff, and so on).
- How does each of these types of pollution affect the sea and its animals and plants?
- What's being done to help solve ocean pollution problems?
- What can people do in their daily lives to lessen some of these problems?

GRAPH 1   INCREASE IN U.S. PLASTIC PRODUCTION

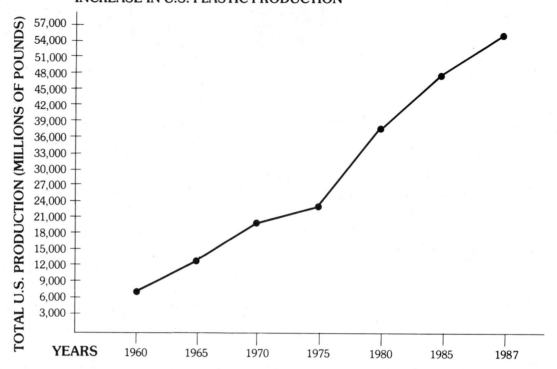

1. During which five-year period did the greatest increase in plastic production occur?

2. Compare the plastic production in 1987 and 1960. How much higher or lower was it in 1987?

3. How much did plastic production increase from 1975 to 1987?

4. Compare graph 1 and 2. Between the years of 1977 and 1987, which graph shows a greater increase? Can you explain why the rate of increase is different between the two graphs?

5. How many millions of pounds of plastic were used to make non-packaging plastic in 1987? Name some other types of plastic products.

6. Given the trends you see in graphs 1 and 2, predict what each graph will look like 10 years from now. What are some factors that might affect plastic production and packaging?

GRAPH 2

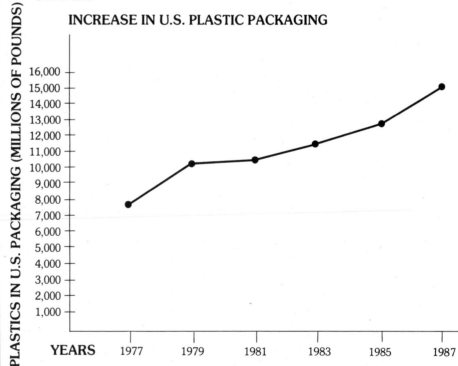

INCREASE IN U.S. PLASTIC PACKAGING

RANGER RICK'S NATURESCOPE: DIVING INTO OCEANS
(See *Plastic in the Sea*—p 59)

- Young seals often play with plastic six-pack rings and get the bands caught around their necks. These bands can strangle them as they grow.

- Over 14 billion pounds of trash is dumped into the ocean every year. A large percentage of this trash is plastic.

- Small pellets, beads, cylinders, and other types of raw plastic are dumped or spilled into the ocean. Seabirds often mistake this plastic for fish eggs, fish eyes, or plankton and sometimes die from eating it.

- Some states have banned non-biodegradable plastic six-pack rings.

- Some plastics contain PCBs—chemicals that cause some birds to lay thin-shelled eggs that break easily.

- Every year, millions of pounds of plastic fishing nets, buoys, lines, and other gear is lost at sea.

- Sea turtles often feed on plastic bags, mistaking them for jellyfish. Many of these turtles eventually starve to death because the plastic clogs their digestive system.

- Over 30,000 northern fur seals die each year after becoming entangled in plastic nets and plastic six-pack rings. They die of strangulation, starvation, drowning, or exhaustion.

- Most plastic is not biodegradable. That means it takes many years for the plastic to break down, or disintegrate.

- Scientists have developed some biodegradable plastics. However, not enough research has been done to know if these biodegradable plastics break down into safe substances.

- Some communities are experimenting with plastic recycling, but it is still very expensive.

- In late 1988, an international treaty took effect that restricts plastic ocean dumping by the nations that ratified it—including the United States.

A Pop-up Coral Reef

Make a 3-D coral reef.

Ages:
*Intermediate and
Advanced*

Materials:
- *copies of page 65*
- *construction paper*
- *scissors*
- *blunt pencils or
  ball-point pens*
- *glue*
- *crayons, markers. or
  colored pencils*
- *rulers*

Subjects:
Arts and Crafts

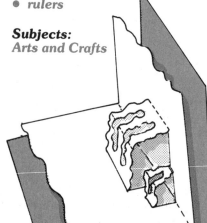

construction paper

This pop-up reef is easy and fun to make. Here's how to do it:

1. Spread a thin film of glue over the back of page 65 and glue it to a sheet of construction paper. (Be sure to cover the *entire sheet* with glue.) Trim away the excess construction paper.

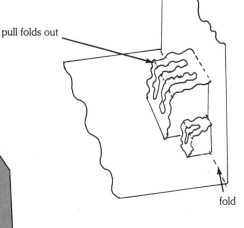

pull folds out

fold

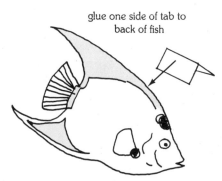

glue one side of tab to back of fish

2. Remove the drawings of the reef animals at both ends of the sheet by cutting along the wavy lines. Set these drawings aside to use later.

3. Score all the dashed lines with a blunt pencil or ball-point pen. Press firmly, but be careful not to tear the paper. (You might want to use a ruler to help you keep your lines straight.)

4. With the printed side facing out, fold the page in half along the dashed line. Crease well with the edge of a pencil or ruler.

5. Cut through both layers of the paper along all the *solid* lines. (You will cut some pieces out completely. But be sure that you don't cut along any dashed lines.)

6. Open the page carefully. Gently pull the cut-out features outward, in the opposite direction that they were originally folded in. Crease each construction paper feature along its folded edges. Then carefully close the pop-up again.

7. Fold a different-colored piece of construction paper in half width-wise. Then glue the fold of the cut-out reef into the fold of the construction paper. Don't put glue on any of the cut-out parts. Trim excess construction paper from the sides only, leaving extra paper at the top and bottom. Close the pop-up, making sure that the cut-out parts are folded out the right way, and put under a heavy book to dry.

8. Color the reef animals you set aside earlier and cut them out.

9. Glue the animals onto your pop-up reef. You can glue some of them to the pop-up part and some to the flat background. To make the reef animals stand out from the background, make a tab by folding a small piece of construction paper in half. The folded tab should be smaller than the animal you are gluing it to so it won't show. Glue one side of the tab to the animal and the other side to the reef. You can add pop-up rocks, different types of coral, or other features to your reef.

Luise Woelflein

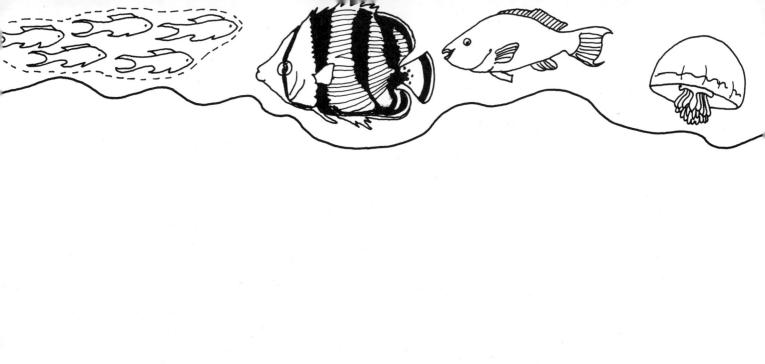
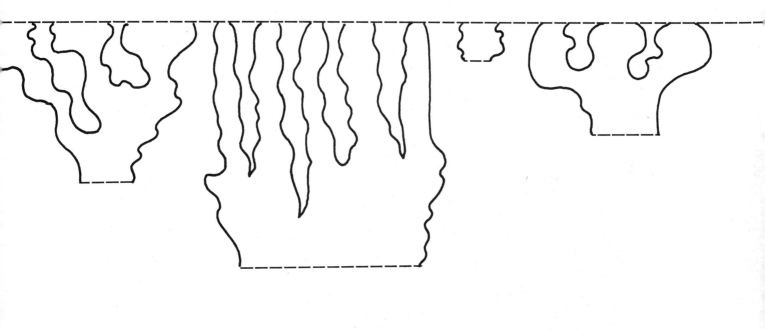
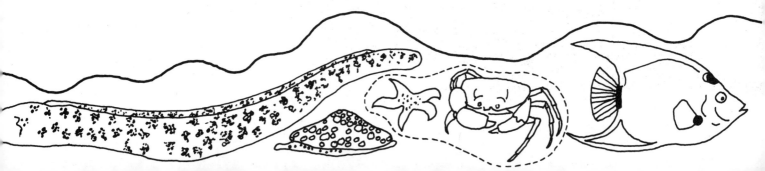

Jazzy Jellyfish

Use paper plates and ribbon to make colorful jellyfish.

Ages:
Primary

Materials:
- *paper plates*
- *thin ribbon*
- *scissors*
- *tape*
- *crayons or markers*
- *pictures of jellyfish*

Subjects:
Arts and Crafts

Your kids will have fun making and playing with these colorful jellyfish. They can hang them up or even wear them on their heads! First show the kids pictures of different kinds of jellyfish. Then have them follow these simple steps:

1. Make the tentacles by cutting thin party ribbon into pieces varying in length from 8 to 18 inches. You will need to cut 30 or more pieces for each jellyfish.
2. Use scissors to curl some of the ribbon "tentacles." Leave some of the pieces straight.
3. Color the paper plate "body" with crayons or markers. Then tape the ribbon tentacles to the inside of the plate (the side you eat from). Tape most of them around the plate's edge, but put a few in the middle. When you turn the plate over, the tentacles will hang down—just like those of a real jellyfish!

Glossary

bioluminescence—the production of light by organisms. Angler fish and lantern fish are examples of ocean animals that are *luminescent*.

echo sounding—a technique that uses sonar to calculate ocean depth and map the ocean floor.

hydrothermal vents—cracks in the Earth's crust along mid-ocean ridges that spew out hot, mineral-rich water. Special deep-sea communities are clustered around these vents in the dark ocean depths.

intertidal zone—the coastal area between the low- and high-tide lines that is alternately covered with water and exposed to the air.

ocean current—a "river of water" that flows in a particular direction.

Surface currents, such as the Gulf Stream, are caused mostly by prevailing winds. *Deep ocean currents* are caused by density differences in ocean water.

ocean floor—the Earth's surface at the bottom of the ocean. It consists of features such as continental shelves, slopes, and rises; mid-ocean ridges; abyssal plains; and deep-sea trenches.

plankton—the collective name for small, drifting plants (*phytoplankton*) and animals (*zooplankton*). These aquatic organisms are the basis of ocean food webs.

prevailing winds—winds that consistently blow in the same general direction and that generate most of the ocean's surface currents. The trade winds and the westerlies are examples of prevailing winds.

salinity—the total amount of dissolved solids in water, generally expressed as the "saltiness" of water.

tide—the periodic ebb and flow of ocean waters caused by the gravitational pull between the Earth and the moon and the Earth and the sun. Along many coasts of the world, there are usually two high tides and two low tides each day.

tide pool—a depression or crevice on a rocky shore that retains water when the tide goes out. Many marine plants and animals live in tide pools.

upwelling—a movement of water that flows up from the deep sea, bringing nutrients to the ocean's surface.

1997 UPDATE

TABLE OF CONTENTS

BE A WATER TREATMENT OFFICER 68

COPYCAT PAGE 70
• The Water Treatment Plant

SALT MARSH SECRETS 71

MARINE POLLUTION: A CRITICAL COASTAL ISSUE 80

• Major Marine Pollutants
• How Pollution Gets into Coastal Waters
• Impacts of Marine Pollution
• Concentration of Contaminants in Marine Organisms
• Nutrient and Organic Enrichment
• Pollution Prevention

CREATURES OF THE SEA 87

CURRENTS 91

OCEANS BIBLIOGRAPHY 92

Be a Water Treatment Officer

Summary:
An experiment to look at the steps and processes involved in purifying water.

Objectives:
Completing this activity will allow students to:
- *Explain the steps and processes involved in purifying water at a water treatment plant*
- *Understand why water must be cleansed and purified before it is safe for human consumption*
- *Discover where the sources of drinking water are in the area*
- *Recognize a career option that connects environmental and health issues in a way that directly benefits society*

Age:
Intermediate

Time:
30-40 minutes

Subjects:
Science, Social Studies, Geography, and Health

When water falls to earth and flows into reservoirs, aquifers, and lakes, it can collect dirt particles, bacteria, and other biological and chemical pollutants. These contaminants must be removed from our water supply before the water is safe to drink. This activity simulates the treatment process water goes through before it flows from our tap.

The United States has one of the best and cleanest drinking water systems in the world. Water treated at the local water treatment facility goes through an extensive process before we drink it. Water is first aerated, by spraying it into the air to release trapped gasses and to absorb oxygen. Next, powdered alum is added to the water. The alum binds with dirt particles, now called "floc," that become heavy and sink to the bottom (sedimentation). The water is then filtered through layers of sand, gravel, and charcoal to remove any remaining small particles. Finally, a small amount of chlorine is added to kill bacteria and micro-organisms.

In rural areas, many homes get their water from wells that tap into the local aquifer. This water is not treated at a water treatment facility. It may contain various dissolved minerals or even biological contaminants, but it usually is safe to drink without treatment. However, all well water should be tested regularly to detect harmful contaminants that may enter the aquifer.

PROCEDURE

1. This activity works well in conjunction with a discussion about aquifers and reservoirs. Ask students if they know the source of their local drinking water. Learn the name of the local reservoir or aquifer, and identify it on a local map. Some students may be revolted at the thought that their drinking water comes from a reservoir where boating and fishing activities also take place. Explain that water is treated before it reaches our faucets. Explain that during this activity they will become "water treatment officers" for a day, and learn how to treat water properly before it is released for consumption. Briefly explain how water is treated before starting the activity.

2. Break the class into groups of two or three students. Distribute *The Water Treatment Plant* Copycat page, and ask students to consider the bucket of dirty water to be the reservoir. Instruct one student from each group to stir the water well and use it to fill one clear plastic cup three-quarters full. Have the other students in the group collect the materials they need and set up the simulation activity. Keep one cup of dirty water as a control to compare to after the water has been treated.

3. Have the students follow the instructions on their *Water Treatment Plant* handout. Offer assistance if needed, supervising the activity as the students carry out their simulation.

EXTENSIONS / MODIFICATIONS

- A simpler version of this activity requires only a coffee filter and a funnel. This will illustrate the way water is filtered without following the more complex instruction in this activity.
- Use the words in this lesson for vocabulary words of the week.
- Read *The Magic School Bus At The Waterworks* By Joanna Cole, or assign the book as homework reading. It reinforces the concepts presented here.
- Take your students on a field trip to see the way a real water treatment plant functions, or take them to the wastewater treatment plant, which handles water from homes, drains, and restrooms. Have a representative from your local water treatment facility speak to your class about water treatment.
- Test various water samples for contamination. Collect samples from the tap water in different locations or a local river, stream, or lake.

Reprinted from the *Animal Tracks Activity Guide* published by The National Wildlife Federation®

INSTRUCTIONS

1. Take one clear plastic cup to the "reservoir" and fill it three-quarters full of water.

Water to be purified

Sand

Gravel

Filter holes

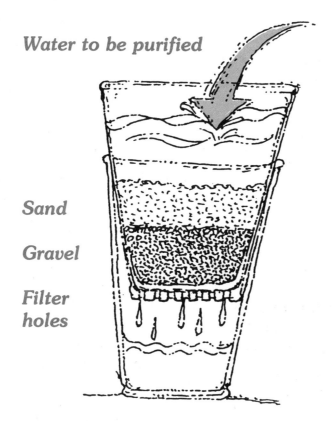

2. Using a pencil, punch eight to ten holes in the bottom of the white foam cup. Place a piece of paper towel or filter paper on the inside of the cup at the bottom. Put one inch of gravel in the cup. Cover the gravel with one inch of sand. Set this filter cup aside.

3. Pour the dirty water in the clear cup into the other clear cup. Repeat two more times. This process is called *aeration*.

4. Take 1/2 tsp. alum and put it into the cup containing the water. The alum will bind to the dirt in the water. This is called *coagulation*. The alum

and dirt are heavy and will form a layer on the bottom of the cup. This is called *sedimentation*.

5. Place an empty cup underneath the white foam cup with the sand and gravel filter. After the particles in the clear cup have fallen to the bottom, pour the water into the white foam cup. This step is called *filtration*. The water coming through the filter is free of dirt.

6. Use the eyedropper to place two drops of the "bleach" into your water. If this were really chlorine, it would kill bacteria and microorganisms in the water. If this were a real water treatment plant, you would now have water clean enough to drink.

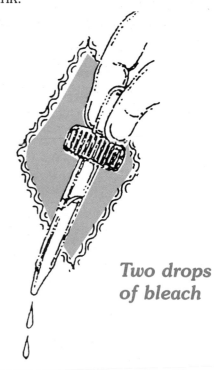

Two drops of bleach

7. When cleaning up, save the water to water plants. Wash the clear plastic cups so they can be used again.

Salt Marsh Secrets

Salt marshes are wonderful places. They are full of secrets and hidden treasures. Many things depend on salt marshes for survival, including humans!

Salt marshes are created by the ocean's influences. They are found along the coastlines. These areas are low and wet and the ground is soft and soggy.

Salt marshes act as a natural filtering system. They help trap trash, sewage waste, and other pollutants that run off from the land.

Healthy salt marshes act as buffers. They help control coastal flooding and erosion.

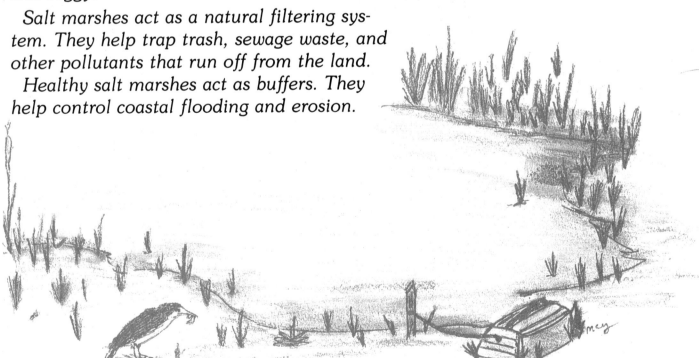

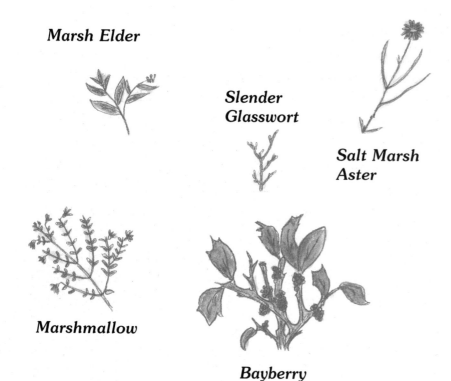

Marsh Elder

Slender Glasswort

Salt Marsh Aster

Marshmallow

Bayberry

Plants are the heart of the salt marsh. They produce oxygen for us to breathe. They provide food and shelter for many animals. These plants also hold back and anchor the soil. This prevents the soil from washing away into the water.

There are many kinds of flowers and shrubs that grow along the edge of the salt marsh.

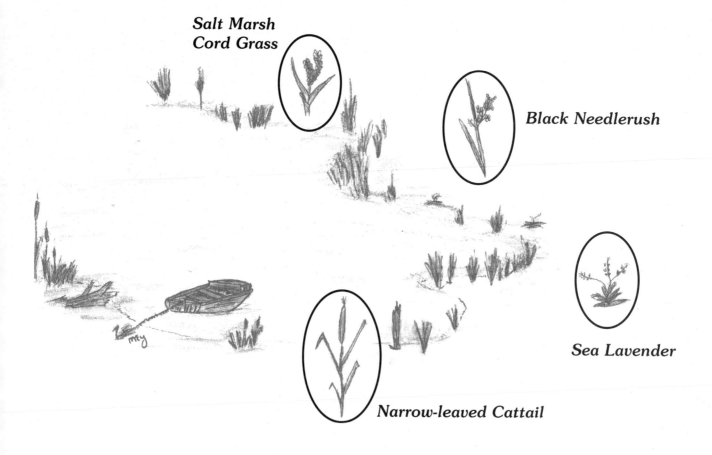

Salt Marsh Cord Grass

Black Needlerush

Sea Lavender

Narrow-leaved Cattail

Hidden deep within the salt marsh grass live salt marsh snails and salt marsh fleas. These little creatures spend their time slithering and hopping up and down the grass to keep from getting wet by the salty tide.

When the tide is low and the mud exposed, out pop the little fiddler crabs. Smaller than an inch, they spend their day fiddling for food. Fiddlers feed on pieces of dead plants and animals.

Fiddlers are also an important food source for blue crabs, raccoons, and many birds.

Male fiddler crabs have one large claw and one small claw. Females have two small claws.

When the tide is high, the fiddlers retreat into their burrows to wait until the mud is exposed again with the next low tide.

The more fiddler crabs around, the healthier the salt marsh is.

Half buried in the lower parts of the salt marsh, lives the ribbed mussel. This two inch, clam-like animal feeds on tiny organisms called plankton, that float in the water. The ribbed mussel helps to filter and clean the water. This little animal can pump and filter more than a gallon of water an hour!

Salt Marsh Flea

Salt Marsh Snail

Fiddler crabs

Ribbed Mussels

Seaside Sparrow

Red-Winged Blackbird

Marsh Wren

Many birds depend on the salt marsh for survival. This sanctuary provides food, shelter, and a place for birds to raise their young.

In return, these birds help reduce the population of many biting insects.

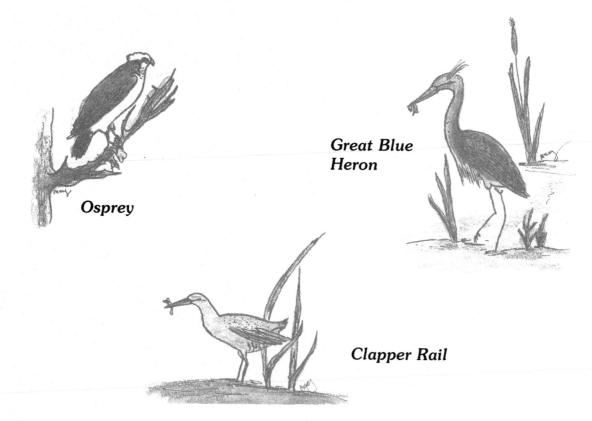

Osprey

Great Blue Heron

Clapper Rail

Other birds depend on the abundance of fish, crabs, and other animals that live in the waters and mud that surround the marsh.

During the spring and fall months, thousands of birds stop to rest in the salt marsh. The tall grasses provide food, protection, and a resting place for tired, migrating birds.

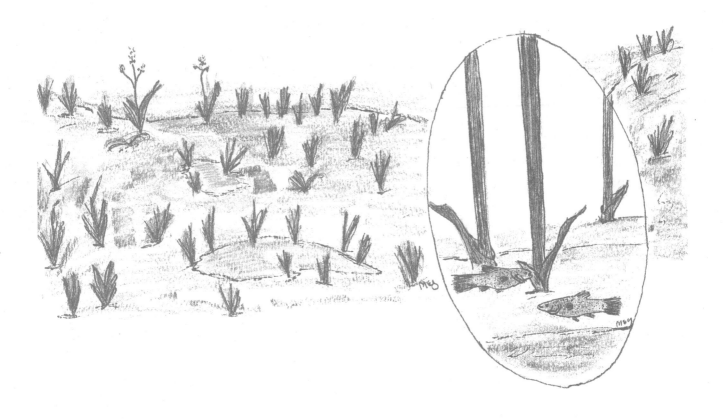

About every six hours, the tides send a change of water to the salt marsh. There are two low and two high tides every day.

During low tide, small pools form in the mud flats. These pools are full of life. Sometimes, fish get trapped in these pools.

While this killifish waits for the next high tide, it will feed on many insect larvae. These fish control the populations of many biting insects.

Striped Bass

Bluefish

When the tide is high again, many animals crawl out of the cool, wet mud and move around searching for food.

High tide brings many visitors from the ocean.

Some fish, like the striped bass, stop to feed on smaller fish and crabs while swimming to their spawning grounds.

Others come in regularly to feed and leave with the next tide.

Adult mullet live and breed in the ocean. However, the young mullet gather and swim into the shallow waters around the marsh. There they feed and grow until they are adults and swim back to the ocean. The salt marsh is their nursery.
The salt marsh is a nursery for many animals and plants.

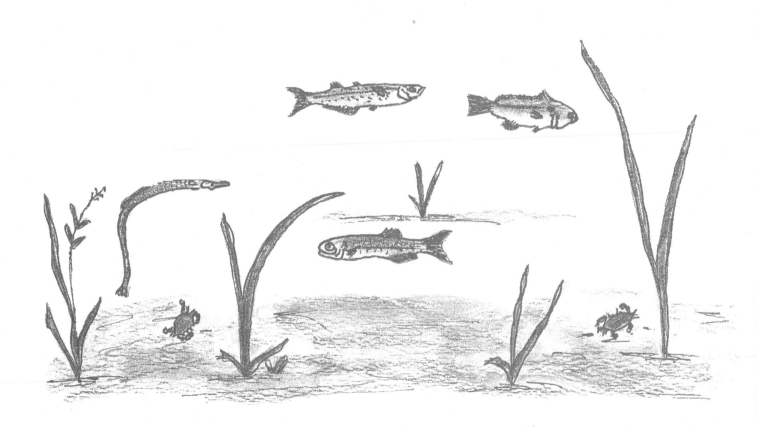

Fishermen also depend on the marsh for survival. Two-thirds of the nation's fisheries depend on the marshes. Many of the ocean fish swim into the salt marsh to spawn (to produce young.) These marshes provide food and shelter so that young fish can grow into big fish. The big fish provide food for us.

The salt marsh is a very special and important place. Many things depend on it for survival. It is important that we look closely for its hidden secrets.

MARINE POLLUTION
A CRITICAL COASTAL ISSUE

The world's oceans have been used for the disposal of wastes produced by businesses and industries, towns and cities, and farms. Population growth, new ways of packaging, and new manufactured materials have all increased the amounts of waste materials that find their way into coastal waters. Pollutants entering our oceans threaten the quality of the marine (saltwater) environment and our ability to use and enjoy its precious resources. However, while scientists have studied ocean pollution, understanding the effect of individual pollutants has been difficult because coastal waters receive many pollutants from a variety of sources.

Major Marine Pollutants

Organic material includes waste from pets, farm animals, and people. Too much organic waste can be harmful to coastal waters. Microscopic organisms (living things too small to see with your naked eye) that decompose organic material use up oxygen in the process. As a result, the oxygen supply in the water may decrease below a level needed by fish and other organisms. This results in the death of marine life.

Nutrients include nitrogen and phosphorus, which are needed for the proper growth and reproduction of plants. But an oversupply of nutrients entering the marine environment from farms and gardens or sewage treatment plants can result in too much growth of microscopic marine plants known as *phytoplankton* (fit-ō-plank-ton). This situation, known as *nutrient enrichment* and *eutrophication* (yoo-tro-fi-kā-shun), may lead to decreased levels of oxygen in the water, which can lead to the death of fish.

Pathogens (organisms that cause disease) include bacteria and viruses that get into the marine environment along with animal and human waste. Some marine animals may eat and retain these pathogens. Although pathogens may not harm these animals, they may cause serious illness in people who eat *them*.

Organic chemicals include pesticides and manufactured chemicals. Not all of these chemicals have an impact on water quality or marine life. However, some of them, such as those used to control insects and other pests (pesticides containing chemicals like Chlordane, Aldrin and Dieldrin), and chemicals known as PCBs (polychlorinated biphenyls) pose a serious threat to the ecosystem since they do not readily break down and can be ingested or absorbed by marine animals.

Heavy metals such as mercury, lead, cadmium (kad-mee-um), and zinc find their way into marine waters from the mining of metal ores and the manufacture of metal objects, paints, dyes, and cloth. Some organisms can pass metals through their bodies or regulate their level of metals. However, as a group, heavy metals are potentially deadly to marine organisms.

Oil is another major pollutant that finds its way into the ocean from a variety of sources including natural seepage and accidental spills.

Silt and sediment includes soil, sand, and rock particles eroded from the land and carried to coastal waves. In shallow water, silt and sediment particles can prevent sunlight from reaching the bottom, killing underwater plants that rely on light to grow. In addition, many pollutants cling to particles of silt and sediment in the water. They are carried to the bottom. Once on the bottom, the contaminants may be eaten by marine organisms.

Solid waste includes plastics, wood, glass, lost fishing gear, packaging materials, and other debris that enters the ocean from littering, human carelessness, and illegal dumping. Clumps of solid waste and debris found in the oceans are referred to as *floatables*. Once floatables wash up on the shoreline, they are referred to as *marine debris*. Marine debris poses a hazard to marine life. Birds and fish can get tangled or stuck in debris. Also, if these animals eat debris, their stomachs can become full or blocked and they may starve.

How Pollution Gets into Coastal Waters

Direct discharges of liquid wastes produced by sewage treatment plants, factories, and businesses are known as point sources. Modern sewage treatment plants can treat waste and eliminate most pollutants. Unfortunately, some cities and towns provide minimal treatment. Wastewater discharged from these facilities still contains sediment particles, nutrients, pathogens, heavy metals, and organic chemicals. In addition, if sewage treatment plants are overloaded, they can discharge untreated sewage.

Stormwater discharges include water that runs into storm sewers and then empties directly to coastal waters. They may contain litter, debris, and other pollutants washed off the land (such as fertilizers and pesticides) or discarded by people (such as used motor oil). In some cities, storm sewers carry their waste to sewage treatment plants. However, in many older cities, sewage treatment plants may not be able to handle the flow from storm sewers when it rains. This situation results in direct discharges of raw sewage, litter, and other pollutants into coastal waters.

Runoff consists of water that flows off streets, parking lots, lawns, farmland, and forests directly into coastal waters. Runoff carries debris, sediment, oil, animal wastes, litter, and other pollutants directly into the water. This varied source of pollution, known collectively as *nonpoint source pollution*, is a major source of nutrients, organic matter, pathogens, and organic chemicals.

Rivers and streams carry soil, sediment, and related pollutants into the marine environment. Wastes and related pollutants that find their way into rivers and streams from the land are eventually carried downstream to bays and to coastal waters.

The atmosphere deposits pollutants in coastal waters from rainfall and fallout of particles such as dust and smoke. Although scientists do not know how much pollution comes from the atmosphere, it may contribute significantly to marine pollution.

Discharges from ships and boats include oil, sewage, and solid waste. These wastes can create hazards to navigation and endanger marine animals.

Accidental spills, although uncommon, can release substantial quantities of oil and other pollutants along the coast. Some large oil spills have wiped out communities of marine organisms and destroyed hundreds of acres of their habitats.

Uncontrolled sources of coastal pollution include churning up of sediments during dredging, chemicals seeping from landfills, and illegal dumping. A large amount of sand, silt, and mud is dredged from waterways in order to keep them open to navigation, and contaminants associated with bottom sediments can be churned up during dredging.

Impacts of Marine Pollution

Although some pollutants may be relatively harmless to the environment and organisms, others may cause serious problems. This makes it difficult to identify and understand the problems caused by pollutants. However, scientists have concluded that the disappearance of certain organisms in some areas are the result of chemical pollutants from land. For example, just 150 years ago oysters were abundant in Raritan Bay, New Jersey, but 50 years later, destruction of seed beds and industrial pollution had caused the end of the oyster industry. During this same period, housing development along the coast of Staten Island, New York, was accompanied by construction of sewage discharge pipes. These point sources contributed to a decline in the number of shellfish species found in the area. Information like this provides evidence that pollution can stress marine organisms and reduce their lifespans and their ability to adapt to their environment.

There is some evidence that diseases in fish and shellfish are associated with pollution. For example, in laboratory studies English sole have lost weight when exposed to chemicals in oil known as petroleum hydrocarbons. Recent studies in the Hudson River, New York, indicate that many Atlantic tomcod have liver tumors and deformities caused by exposure to chemical pollutants.

Fin rot is a condition caused by pollutants that affects the structure of a fish's fins. Fish suffering from fin rot become less fit to swim and capture their food. Lobsters, crabs, and shrimp may be affected by erosion of their outer skeleton. Although this condition, known as shell disease, can occur naturally, it is more widespread and severe in polluted areas.

Concentration of Contaminants in Marine Organisms

Organisms exposed to pollutants may absorb contaminants or eat them. This process is known as *bioaccumulation* (bi-o-a-kyoom-yu-lā-shen). As organisms feed, the pollution levels in their body may become higher. This process is known as *biomagnification* (bi-o-mag-ne-fi-kā-shen). As a result of biomagnification, pollutant levels in organisms at the top of the food chain may be many times higher than those at lower levels.

Some fish and shellfish harvested by fishermen have accumulated chemical contaminants in their tissues, and there is concern that eating them may pose a health risk to people. As a result, there are health advisories on eating fish caught in some areas. For example, New York has banned the commercial harvest of striped bass from the Hudson River. New York and New Jersey have issued advisories warning sport fishers to limit consumption of bluefish, striped bass, and American eels that they catch in the Hudson-Raritan Estuary.

Clams and other shellfish may eat and concentrate bacteria and other pathogens from the water as they feed. If people eat these shellfish, they may become extremely ill. If high levels of bacteria are found in areas containing shellfish beds, they are closed and fishermen cannot harvest them. In some regions, shellfish from closed areas are taken to areas with clean water to allow them to rid themselves of contaminants by filtering clean water through their bodies. This process is known as *depuration* (dep-ye-rā-shen).

Nutrient and Organic Enrichment

Excessive nutrients result in a condition known as eutrophication. Eutrophication often leads to the growth of so much algae that it produces an "algae bloom." Blooms are sometimes referred to as red, green, or brown tides because they discolor the water.

Some algae blooms merely affect appearance, such as water discoloration. Some algae species, such as those responsible for red tides, can produce natural poisons that become concentrated in shellfish and can affect people if they eat these shellfish. When algae blooms die, they fall to the bottom and consume oxygen as the dead algae is decomposed. Even if fish don't die as a result bottom-dwelling organisms like crabs and clams do.

Pollution Prevention

Important federal laws related to marine pollution are the Marine Protection, Research, and Sanctuaries Act; the Clean Water Act; and the Marine Plastics Pollution Research and Control Act. These and other federal and state laws are designed to regulate and control the disposal of all types of waste materials in coastal and ocean waters. However, despite these laws, beaches still close, algae blooms, fish are killed, habitats and organisms are contaminated, and uncontrolled coastal development continues.

Everyone can help prevent pollution by (1) properly disposing of waste products, including picking up pet waste and disposing of it in the trash, (2) reducing the use of toxic household products by purchasing environmentally sound products, (3) recycling everything from plastic, glass, cardboard, and paper, to used motor oil, (4) minimizing the use of fertilizers and pesticides, and (5) using water wisely.

Types, Sources, and Effects of Major Pollutants

Type of Pollutant	Primary Sources
Organic Matter	Animal and human waste; Runoff
Nutrients	Fertilizer runoff, Sewage discharges
Pathogens	Animal and human waste; Runoff
Organic Chemicals	Agricultural runoff; Industrial waste
Heavy Metals	Industrial waste; Runoff
Oil and Petroleum Hydrocarbons	Discharges from ships; Spills, Runoff
Silt and Sediment	Erosion; Runoff; Rivers
Solid Waste	Litter; Vessels; Runoff

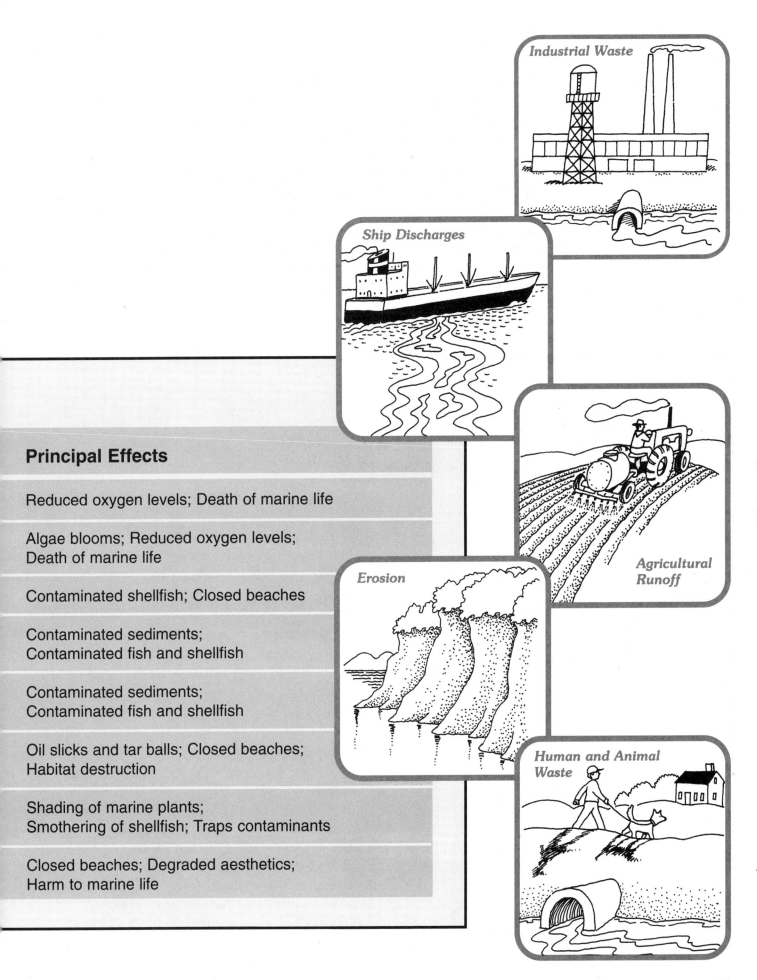

Industrial Waste

Ship Discharges

Agricultural Runoff

Erosion

Human and Animal Waste

Principal Effects

Reduced oxygen levels; Death of marine life

Algae blooms; Reduced oxygen levels;
Death of marine life

Contaminated shellfish; Closed beaches

Contaminated sediments;
Contaminated fish and shellfish

Contaminated sediments;
Contaminated fish and shellfish

Oil slicks and tar balls; Closed beaches;
Habitat destruction

Shading of marine plants;
Smothering of shellfish; Traps contaminants

Closed beaches; Degraded aesthetics;
Harm to marine life

Clean Ocean Action's
Ten Tips For Students

READ
Keep informed on environmental issues by reading newspapers and magazines.

WRITE
Contact politicians, lawmakers, and polluters to let them know you're watching.

REDUCE
Cut down on the amount of trash you produce. In school, use both side of writing paper.

REUSE
Buy products that are reusable such as pens and pencils, sandwich containers, drink containers,
and canvas lunch bags.

RECYCLE
Follow your school's recycling rules. Encourage your school to buy recycled paper.
Start a composting pile on school grounds.

RID
Rid your school of toxics. Encourage your school to use "Integrated Pest Management," a method of pest control
that uses chemical toxins only as a last resort.

GET INVOLVED
Join your school's environmental club or join an environmental organization outside school.

CONSERVE ENERGY
Walk, ride your bike, carpool, or take the bus to school.

ACT LOCALLY
Organize a clean-up of your school grounds, plant a garden, institute recycling and composting in your classroom.

SPREAD THE WORD
Inform your peers about the importance of environmental issues.

Source: Clean Ocean Action, P.O. Box 505, Sandy Hook, NJ 07732

Activity

Ask students to generate a list of human activities that may threaten ocean life. One threatening activity might be an oil spill. This activity will help students to think about the difficulty of cleaning up an oil spill. Gather an aluminum pie plate, salt water, and vegetable oil with food coloring. Fill the pie plate with water. Place 5 drops of oil on the water. Ask students to predict how easily the oil may be separated from the water and to suggest materials that could be used to do it. Using materials available, such as cotton, straw, fake fur, feathers, detergent, or other materials that the students want to experiment with, try to remove the oil from the water. Observe the reaction that the oil has to the cleaning efforts. Record what happens. Does the oil spread out? Does it cling to the cleaning material? Can the oil be contained in a small space? Keep track of the amount of time it takes to clean up the oil spill using different methods. Which techniques seemed to work the best? What effect did detergent have on the oil? What happened when a feather was used? What might this tell us about the effects of oil spills on birds? Fire is another method of cleaning up an oil spill. Where does the oil go when it burns? What kind of problems might this cause? When oil reaches the shoreline, what other problems might occur?

CREATURES OF THE SEA

The bulk of life in the sea is concentrated in those waters that have some access to the sun: the shallow seabed near the shore and the sunlit open sea, 200-300 feet beneath the surface waters.

Life abounds along the edges of the sea, where ridges and hollows form tide pools and reef communities exist. The oldest, most complex, and most tightly integrated ecosystem on the planet exists in ocean reef communities, offshore masses of organic limestone either closely surrounding an island, separated from an island by a lagoon, or enclosing a central lagoon. Never much deeper than 60 feet, coral reefs provide an environment for one-third of all fish in the sea.

Another large portion of the animal life in the sea is concentrated on the world's continental shelves, land extending into the sea to a depth of some 600 feet. The sun's energy is used here to produce nourishment for animal life.

In addition, there is the life of the open sea and the deep sea, known as the abyss. Alternating between scarcity and abundance, schools of fish migrate and wander in the open sea. In the deep sea, with its ice cold water and water pressure 1,000 times greater than atmospheric pressure, specialized animals have adapted to life without sunlight.

One of the most intriguing creatures of the sea has historically been the shark. Sharks are one of the oldest animals that still exist on earth. The shark first appeared about 350 million years ago, predating dinosaurs! Sharks come in all sizes, from the six-inch dwarf shark to the whale shark, which can measure up to 60 feet. There are sharks in every

ocean, both in warm and cold waters. One species can even inhabit rivers and freshwater lakes.

Sharks differ from other fish in a few major ways. Although most fish have skeletons made up of bones, a shark is made of cartilage, a material similar to people's noses and ears. This cartilage skeleton allows the shark to twist and turn with ease. Unlike fish which lay eggs that are fertilized once in the water, most sharks produce eggs that are fertilized and grow inside the mother. Amazingly, almost all shark pups survive.

Sharks are one of the most feared animals on earth. Most of this fear, however, is unfounded. Sharks rarely attack humans. The odds of being hit by lightning, not once but three times, are greater than the odds for being bitten by a shark once!

Whales look like fish, but are actually more closely related to people. They give live birth, nurse their young, and show tenderness toward their calves. They breathe air using nostrils that have evolved to the top of their heads.

Whales are intelligent, warm-blooded marine mammals inhabiting all oceans of the world. Like sharks, there are several freshwater species that live in rivers too. Up to 78 species have been identified including

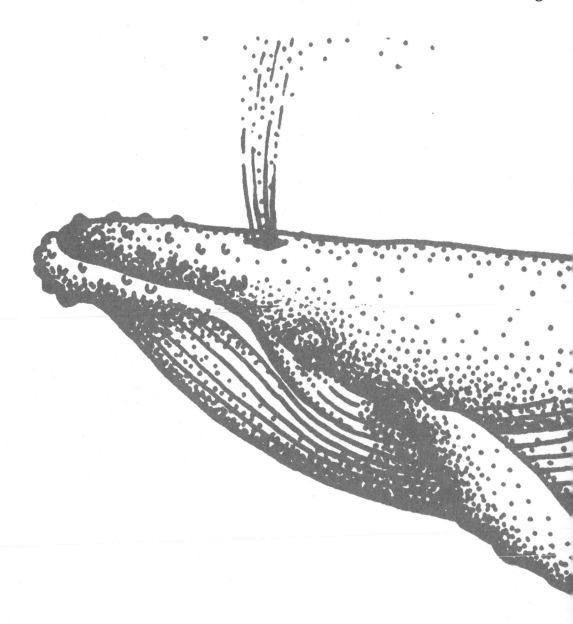

all animals in a group called cetaceans. The best known cetaceans are whales, dolphins, and porpoises.

Even though whales, dolphins, and porpoises look like fish, there is one quick way to tell the difference. Cetacean tails are horizontal and swing up and down; fish tails are vertical and swing from side to side.

ACTIVITIES / DISCUSSION

1. Divide students into five groups. Have each group research the creatures that live in one of the five areas of the ocean: tide pools, the reef community, the continental shelf, the open sea, and the deep sea. Ask student groups to produce a mural illustrating life in each of these environments.

2. Divide students into small groups. Supply them with a ball of string and a yardstick. Ask each group to choose a specific whale, dolphin, or porpoise. Have them record the shape and size of their creature. Instruct them to first sketch their cetacea (whale, dolphin, or porpoise) to get a feel for the general shape.

Then, have them enlarge the shape to scale on the floor. Have them sit inside the shape. How many students would fit inside the creature? Have students choose other objects and estimate how many would fit inside.

3. Using a map of the world, chart the movement of the North Pacific Blue Whale. The National Marine Fisheries Service sitings are listed below. Chart them. After marking the path that the North Pacific Blue Whale takes during the year, compare that path with ocean currents and trade winds. If you wanted to observe the blue whale, where you would visit and when?

Month	Latitude/Longitude	Notes
Jan/Feb	10°N/98°W	Wintering Grounds
Mar/April	28°N/116°N	Spring Migration
May	41°N/130°W	Spring Migration
June	50°N/130°W	Resting
July/August	57°N/130°W	Fall Migration
September	50°N/130°W	Fall Migration
October	36°N/128°W	Fall Migration
November	25°N/115°W	Fall Migration

4. Create class "whale sightings." Ask students to draw their own whale tail. Encourage them to use their imaginations with the design and markings. Have them name their whale. Give each student a 4x6 card to draw their whale tail and name. Place the whale tails on a bulletin board in the room. Then have students draw their tails again and place them somewhere in the school. Encourage the class to find and identify each other's whales. Have students write stories about their whale and the problems it faced as it migrated around the school.

Center for Global Environmental Education
  Hamline University
  1536 Hewitt Avenue
  St. Paul, MN 55104-1248
  phone: 612-523-2480
  e-mail: cgee@gw.hamline.edu
  web site: cgee.hamline.edu

Currents

1. Using an encyclopedia or weather book as a resource, diagram the warm and cold ocean currents of the world. Imagine that you have thrown a message in a bottle into the ocean at some point. Trace with your finger where it might go if it were at the mercy of the currents.

2. Demonstrate how the ocean currents move. Use a dish of water and baby powder. Sprinkle the baby powder over the water surface and then gently blow on the surface. The water will start to move and the powder will start to swirl around in two circles—one turning clockwise and the other counter-clockwise. Compare what happens with a diagram of the Gulf Stream How would life change for the people in Great Britain if there were no currents bringing warm water to their shores?

Center for Global Environmental Education, Hamline University

Oceans Bibliography

Note: A* at the end of a listing indicates that the book is a good source of ocean pictures.

GENERAL REFERENCE BOOKS

Chesapeake Bay: Introduction to an Ecosystem (U.S. Environmental Protection Agency, 1995)

The Encyclopedia of Aquatic Life edited by Keith Banister and Andrew Campbell (Facts on File, 1985)

Exploring Ocean Science, 2nd ed., by Keith Stowe (Wiley, 1995)*

Life in the Chesapeake Bay by A.J. Lippson and R.L. Lippson (Johns Hopkins University Press, 1989)

A Nation of Oceans by Michael Weber and Richard Tinney (Center for Environmental Education, 1986)

Seashore by Steve Parker (Knopf, 1989)*

Turning the Tide by T. Horton and W.M. Eichbaum (Island Press, 1991)

The Undersea Predators by Carl Roessler (Facts on File, 1984)

Under the Sea by The Nature Company Discoveries Library (Time-Life, 1995)*

FIELD GUIDES

The Audubon Society Field Guide to North American Seashells by Harold A. Rehder (Knopf, 1981)*

A Field Guide to the Atlantic Seashore by Kenneth L. Gosner (Houghton Mifflin, 1982)*

A Field Guide to the Birds by R.T. Peterson (Houghton Mifflin., 1947)

Field Guide to the Birds of North America (National Geographic Society, 1992)

Ocean Life is a Nature Finder identification wheel. By turning the wheel, information about different ocean creatures is displayed through windows. Available from Hubbard Scientific. 1-800-446-8767.

Peterson First Guides: Shells by Jackie Leatherbury Douglas (Houghton Mifflin, 1989)*

Shells by S. Peter Dance (Dorling Kindersley, 1992)*

CHILDREN'S BOOKS

Animals That Live in the Sea by Joan Ann Straker (National Geographic Society, 1978). Primary and Intermediate

Coral Reef by Barbara Taylor (Dorling Kindersley, 1992). Primary and IntermediateY

Coral Reefs by Sylvia A. Johnson (Lerner, 1984). Intermediate and Advanced

The Crab on the Seashore by Jennifer Coldrey (Stevens, 1987). Intermediate

A Day in the Life of a Marine Biologist by William Jaspersohn (Little, Brown, 1982). Advanced

Exploring an Ocean Tide Pool by Jeanne Bendick (Holt, 1992). Primary and Intermediate

How to Hide an Octopus and Other Sea Creatures by Ruth Heller (Putnam, 1992). Primary

I Wonder Why the Sea Is Salty and Other Questions About the Oceans by Anita Ganeri (Kingfisher, 1995). Primary and Intermediate

Into the Sea by Brenda Guiberson (Holt, 1996). Primary

Life and Death of the Salt Marsh by J. Teal and M. Teal (Little, Brown, 1969)

Life at the Seashore by Helen Mason (Durkin Hayes, 1990). Primary

The Magic School Bus on the Ocean Floor by Joanna Cole (Scholastic, 1992). Primary and Intermediate

Nature Hide-and-Seek—Oceans by John Norris Wood (Knopf, 1985). Intermediate and Advanced

Questions and Answers About Seashore Animals by Michael Chiney (Kingfisher, 1994). Intermediate

Ranger Rick's Science Spectacular: The Mighty Ocean by Melvin Berger, is part of the Science Spectacular series (Newbridge Communications, 1996). Primary and Intermediate. Call 1-800-347-7829 to subscribe to the series.

Sea Animals by Angela Royston (Dorling Kindersley, 1992). Primary*

The Sea is Calling Me is a collection of poems edited by Lee Bennett Hopkins (Harcourt, Brace, Jovanovich, 1986). Intermediate and Advanced

Seas and Oceans is a series of books about different seas and oceans. (Silver Burdett, 1980). Intermediate

Sea Shells by Jason Cooper (Rourke, 1992). Primary

Shells by Jennifer Coldrey (Dorling Kindersley, 1993). Primary and Intermediate*

Shoreline by Barbara Taylor (Dorling Kindersley, 1993). Intermediate*

Starfish, Seashells, and Crabs by George S. Fichter (Golden, 1993). Primary

Strange Animals of the Sea is a pop-up book

(National Geographic Society, 1987). All ages
A Swim Through the Sea by Kristin Joy Pratt
(Dawn Publications, 1994). Primary and Intermediate
When the Tide is Low by Sheila Cole (Lothrop, Lee
& Shepard, 1985). Primary

FILMS, FILMSTRIPS, SLIDES, AND VIDEOS

Bullfrog Films offers numerous ocean titles. ***The Intertidal Zone*** (Intermediate and Advanced) profiles a unique marine habitat, ***The Shoreline Doesn't Stop Here Anymore*** (Advanced) deals with beach erosion, and ***Troubled Waters: Plastic in the Marine Environment*** (Intermediate and Advanced) deals with ocean pollution. Call 1-800-543-3764 for a catalog.

Coastlines (Intermediate and Advanced) and ***Ecology of the Coral Reef*** (Advanced) are videos available from Films for the Humanities, P.O. Box 2053, Princeton, NJ 08543-2053.

The Great Whales: Endangered Monarchs of the Deep is a filmstrip with cassette for advanced students. Knowledge Unlimited, Box 52, Madison, WI 53701-0052.

National Geographic Society has several ocean-related titles. ***Eye on the Environment: Coral Reefs*** is a poster set including three posters with a teacher's guide for all ages. ***Whales*** is a Wonders of Learning Kit containing 30 student booklets, teacher's guide, activity sheets, and read-along cassettes for primary students. ***World Ocean Floors*** is a series of relief maps showing the Arctic, Atlantic, Indian, and Pacific Oceans. ***The Living Ocean*** (Advanced) is a video on how oceans were formed and how animals live in ocean habitats. ***Portrait of a Whale*** and ***Dolphins*** are videos appropriate for all ages. The Life in the Sea series contains three separate videos for all ages: ***Survival!, Locomotion in the Ocean***, and ***Web of Life***. The video ***Voyage of the Loggerhead*** follows a baby sea turtle during the first 18 months of her life (Intermediate and Advanced). ***Let's Explore a Seashore*** is a video also appropriate for Intermediate and Advanced students. ***Deep Sea Dive*** is one of the Really Wild Animals series of videos for all ages. In addition, many of National Geographic's television specials are also available on video. For catalogs and more information call 1-800-368-2728.

Oceans: Earth's Last Frontier is a video from Rainbow Education Media, 3043 Barrow Dr., Raleigh, NC 27604-3036. Intermediate and Advanced

GAMES AND EDUCATIONAL TOYS

The Nature Company Fishes and Other Sea Creatures in Their Environments by Frances and Charles P. Stewart, III (The Nature Company, 1995). Primary and Intermediate. This book contains text and stickers with ocean backgrounds.

Oceans: A Fact-filled Coloring Book by Diane M. Tyler and James C. Tyler, Ph.D. (Running Press, 1990)

The Prehistoric Ocean: An Explorer's Kit (Running Press, 1996).

Under the Sea by Jennifer Dussling (Grosset &

Dunlap, 1995). Intermediate. This book is a poster with stickers and text.

COMPUTER AND ON-LINE RESOURCES

Discovery Channel Online features many Discovery Channel and The Learning Channel programs, including several relating to marine science. A special school area for teachers contains information on how to obtain videos and other educational materials. The address is http://www.discovery.com

The ***Monterey Bay Aquarium*** has an extensive Web site containing information about current exhibits as well as educational activities to download. Its gift and book store lists books and videos on many ocean topics. The site is at http://www.mbayaq.org/

Ocean Explorers is a CD-ROM featuring several educational activities based on ocean themes. Children can learn the alphabet and colors and identify sea creatures in a few of the several games on this disk (Compton's NewMedia, 1995). Primary

Ocean Planet is a CD-ROM that takes users to the ocean floor to explore its depths. The program contains numerous articles and movies covering ocean life, weather and water patterns, ecology, and many other topics. A special area allows users to ask scientists questions in their fields of expertise. Produced by the Discovery Channel and the Smithsonian Institution/Times Mirror. 1995. Advanced

Ocean Voyager: A Smithsonian Ocean Planet Product is a CD-ROM that allows kids to take an ocean voyage in their own sub. They navigate undersea as they explore the ocean, meet marine creatures, and help clean up toxic wastes. Intermediate and Advanced

Smithsonian Online brings the resources of the Smithsonian Institution to teachers over the Internet. By accessing the Smithsonian's Web page, teachers can find materials specifically for elementary and secondary grades, including photos that can be downloaded and reprints of articles, including "Blue Whale," "Fishes: General," "Estuary Chesapeake Guidebook," "Exploring the Chesapeake at the Smithsonian," and "Blue Planet." The address for the Web page is http://www.si.edu/ The National Museum of Natural History has its own Web site: http://nmnhwww.si.edu/nmnhweb.html You can also access Smithsonian Online over America Online.

Whales of the World is an online educational program for primary and intermediate students. The site features 11 activities, photos, facts, and both a student guide and teacher's guide. Access the site at the International Wildlife Coalition's Web page, under the heading Kid Stuff. The address is http://www.webcom.com/%7Eiwcwww/wurld_wild_web/marine.html

OTHER ACTIVITY SOURCES

American Educational Products offers several oceanography teaching aids suitable for advanced students, including books, maps, videos, and transparencies. To obtain a catalog, call 1-800-446-8767.

Janice Van Cleave's Oceans for Every Kid: Easy Activities That Make Learning Science Fun (Wiley, 1996). Intermediate and Advanced

National Aquarium in Baltimore has an exten-

sive activity guide called **Living in Water** (Intermediate and Advanced). It contains background information, activities, ready-to-copy pages, and a glossary. For more information and a list of publications write National Aquarium in Baltimore, Education Department, Pier 3, 501 E. Pratt St., Baltimore, MD 21202. 1-410-576-3670.

The National Oceanic and Atmospheric Administration (NOAA) of the U.S. Department of Commerce publishes several items of interest to teachers. **Coastal Awareness: A Resource Guide for Teachers** contains background information, activities, and extensive resources. It is available in three different levels: elementary, junior high, and senior high. The **Marine Debris Coloring Book** contains coloring pages and activities for primary and intermediate students. **The Ways of Water Tour Guide** contains tips for exploring local watersheds. In addition, NOAA offers free information on the 14 U.S. marine sanctuaries, including location, features, and available educational materials. Teachers may request any of these items or more information from NOAA's Public Affairs Correspondence Unit, 1305 East-West Hwy., Station 8624, Silver Spring, MD 20910; 1-301-713-3145; or visit their Web site at http://www.nos.noaa.gov/ocrm/

The National Science Teachers Association (NSTA) has **Project Earth Science: Physical Oceanography** (Intermediate and Advanced), containing background information and 18 activities focusing on how ocean water affects the Earth and the forces that cause currents, waves, and tides. **The Ocean Book: Aquarium and Seaside Activities and Ideas for All Ages** is NSTA's activity guide containing experiments, puzzles, games, and investigations into the marine world. **Oceanography** is the first volume of the Whales in the Classroom series. It introduces sea geology, biology in ocean inhabitants, and the ecology of oceans to intermediate and advanced students. For more information and to order call NSTA at 1-800-722-NSTA.

Project WILD Aquatic Education Activity Guide contains many ocean and water-related activities for all ages. For more information write Project WILD, 5430 Grosvenor Lane, Bethesda, MD 20814. Or visit their Web site at http://www.eelink.umich.edu/wild/ **Wavelets** are handouts on different ocean topics. Each one contains background information on the topic, and may include a game, puzzle, or activity. Available as a set of 27 for a minimal charge. For a list of these and other marine publications write Sea Grant Communications, Virginia Institute of Marine Science, Gloucester Point, VA 23062. 1-804-642-7170.

WHERE TO GET MORE INFORMATION

- aquariums and oceanariums
- college and university departments of marine science or oceanography
- maritime museums
- ocean magazines such as Dolphin Log and Sea Frontiers
- state departments of marine resources
- state Sea Grant program headquarters

Internet Address Disclaimer

The Internet information provided here was correct, to the best of our knowledge, at the time of publication. It is important to remember, however, the dynamic nature of the Internet.

Resources that are free and publicly available one day may require a fee or restrict access the next, and the location of items may change as menus and homepages are reorganized.

Natural Resources

Ranger Rick, published by the National Wildlife Federation, is a monthly nature magazine for elementary-age children.

Ranger Rick magazine is an excellent source of additional information and activities on dinosaurs and many other aspects of nature, outdoor adventure, and the environment. This 48-page award-winning monthly publication of the National Wildlife Federation is packed with the highest-quality color photos, illustrations, and both fiction and nonfiction articles. All factual information in **Ranger Rick** has been checked for accuracy by experts in the field. The articles, games, puzzles, photo-stories, crafts, and other features inform as well as entertain and can easily be adapted for classroom use. To order or for more information, call 1-800-588-1650.

The EarthSavers Club provides an excellent opportunity for you and your students to join thousands of others across the country in helping to improve our environment. Sponsored by Target Stores and the National Wildlife Federation, this program provides children aged 6 to 14 and their adult leaders with free copies of the award-winning **EarthSavers** newspaper and **Activity Guide** four times during the school year, along with a leader's handbook, EarthSavers Club certificate, and membership cards. For more information on how to join, call 1-703-790-4535 or write to EarthSavers; National Wildlife Federation; 8925 Leesburg Pike; Vienna, VA 22184.